CW01367774

Design on the Elizabeth line

Edited by James Whiting

First Published 2023
Reprinted 2024

Published by Capital Transport Publishing Ltd

www.capitaltransport.com

Printed by Parksons Graphics

Capital Transport

Contents

Crossrail

John Glover

On 23 February 2016 HM Queen Elizabeth II visited the Crossrail construction works at Bond Street to hear the then Mayor of London, Boris Johnson, announce that the project would be renamed the Elizabeth line in her honour. Another name suggested was Churchill line. The working name was Crossrail, or Crossrail 1 when Crossrail 2 became a possibility. These names are sometimes used in this book. Her Majesty formally opened the Elizabeth line at Paddington on 18 May 2022, with public services to and from Abbey Wood starting six days later on Tuesday 24 May.

The lack of east-west communications within the capital was always seen as a serious shortcoming. In 1863 an underground rail link was opened by the Metropolitan Railway between Paddington and the City. This was built using the cut-and-cover construction method and was powered by steam traction. This gave passengers from the Great Western Railway a much desired railway route over the intervening 4.3 miles, though they mostly had to change trains.

One hundred years later, London Underground traffic as a whole could be divided into broadly three groups. The first was that from (mostly) Greater London origins into the centre of London, typical commuter traffic and accounting for about 40% of the total Underground patronage. Another 40% was that which originated on National Rail, maybe from a rather greater distance out, but again aimed at Central London destinations. For the most part, London Underground would only be carrying such passengers within Zone 1, to use a present day term. The Underground would also be remunerated accordingly in the fares receipts. Also in this group would be ordinary movements which were not part of a longer distance journey. The third group of around 20% was those whose Underground journeys were entirely within Zones 2 to 6, and would thus have no involvement with the Central Zone 1 at all.

It is easy to see how crowding on the Underground would become a particular problem within the central Zone 1, given that the main line London termini were located on the outskirts of the central area. Many were along the Euston Road and its extensions, or close to the Thames either north or south of the river.

One problem was the use of any additional capacity. Might it be seen as a route for long distance passenger traffic (and if so from where to where?), a means of getting National Rail suburban passengers beyond the London termini and in effect to their final central London destination, or was it for traffic that could be considered local in all senses? Each would require a different approach; users of InterCity-type services were unlikely to be satisfied with high density suburban rolling stock, without restaurant facilities, lavatories or luggage space, and no seat reservations.

Matters stood still and in 1974 a London Rail study (otherwise known as the Barran Report) was published. This was a joint effort by the Department of the Environment, the Greater London Council, the British Railways Board and the London Transport Executive. In short, the objective was to examine 'what we should be doing'. It endorsed what would later become Thameslink and the principles of what became the Jubilee line, but seemed rather taken aback by a scheme proposed by British Rail, which employed the first use of the term Crossrail.

Under this scheme, trains would run from somewhere west of Paddington to somewhere east of Liverpool Street. The intermediate stations would be at Marble Arch, Bond Street, Leicester Square and Holborn. At Leicester Square there would be easy interchange with a second line from somewhere south of Victoria to somewhere south of London Bridge with stations also at Green Park, Blackfriars and Monument. The report describes it as 'an exciting and imaginative solution to the problems of overcrowding', but it would clearly be very costly so a feasibility study was recommended.

Time passed, but the situation failed to improve. In March 1988 the then Secretary of State Paul Channon set up the Central London Rail Study, which reported in January 1989. Besides a major upgrading programme, the clearly identified major network addition was that now termed West-East Crossrail route. This would run from west of Paddington in tunnelled section to Bond Street, Tottenham Court Road, Holborn (a station later discarded), Farringdon and Liverpool Street, then out towards Shenfield. This included the proposition for a new western Crossrail branch, running west underground from Bond Street via Marylebone and then mostly on existing alignments to Harrow-on-the-Hill and then stations to Amersham and Aylesbury.

Below The line colour originally chosen for Crossrail was green, but this was subsequently adopted instead for the Croydon Tramlink service.

Right An early idea for the decor of the platforms. At the time, the whole project was seen as a joint London Underground and National Rail operation, which probably explains the absence of roundel name signs in this design.

In 1990, the Government gave the go-ahead to London Underground Ltd and the British Railways Board to develop Crossrail. So far, so good, and on 27 November 1991 the Crossrail Bill was published. It was submitted to Parliament. and the Crossrail 2 route safeguarded. This latter, sometimes referred to as the Chelsea-Hackney line, was seen as complementing the main Crossrail route but on a South West to North East alignment.

The Bill's preliminaries reaffirmed the West-East scheme, with the western addition now to diverge at Old Oak Common with a new underground railway to join the Chiltern line, plus another route from Hayes to Heathrow Airport to complement that authorised by the Heathrow Express Railway Act of 1991.

At this stage, services were expected to run at 24 trains per hour maximum through the central section of Crossrail and at 12tph on the Aylesbury route. Towards Reading there would be 10tph, the remaining 2tph running to the Central Terminal Area (now T2, T3) at Heathrow. Trains might be of 8-cars or 12-cars of 23m vehicles. These would require platform lengths of 190m or 283m; by comparison Underground platform lengths were then a maximum of 140m.

But it all proved to be a false start and in 1994 the Crossrail Bill, promoted by London Regional Transport, was rejected by Parliament. Reasons were not given, but unconfirmed reports suggested that the tail off in City employment in the late 1980s made it unnecessary. Officially, it was on the grounds that the case for the Bill had not been made and there had been 314 petitions against it. Despite this, the route alignment in central London was safeguarded.

The Government cited the constraints on public finances and in April 1996 Sir George Young, then Secretary of State, said that Crossrail could only come about when priority items such as the Underground's Jubilee line extension, Thameslink and the Channel Tunnel Rail Link had been dealt with.

In January 2002, Cross London Rail Links Ltd was established as a joint venture between the Strategic Rail Authority and Transport for London, to see if new life could be injected into the Crossrail project.

It soon became clear that the idea of the main section through central London had now been more or less confirmed. There was still considerable disagreement about the extensions at both ends.

Left The original proposal for the new Tottenham Court Road station building on the corner of Oxford Street and Charing Cross Road.

Below One 1990s idea for a circulating area at Farringdon station, the animal motifs referring to the adjacent Smithfield market.

CROSSRAIL OPTIONS IN THE MONTAGUE REPORT, 2004

This map is based on options shown in the Montague Report. An earlier option for the western leg was to Aylesbury via Harrow and Amersham. There had also been a short-lived plan to have a station at Holborn. Some stations on the eastern and western legs are omitted and there were some decisions to be made about which of these to serve. At Acton there was another short-lived plan to divert before Acton Main Line to serve Acton Central, a diversion that would have required the building of a viaduct.

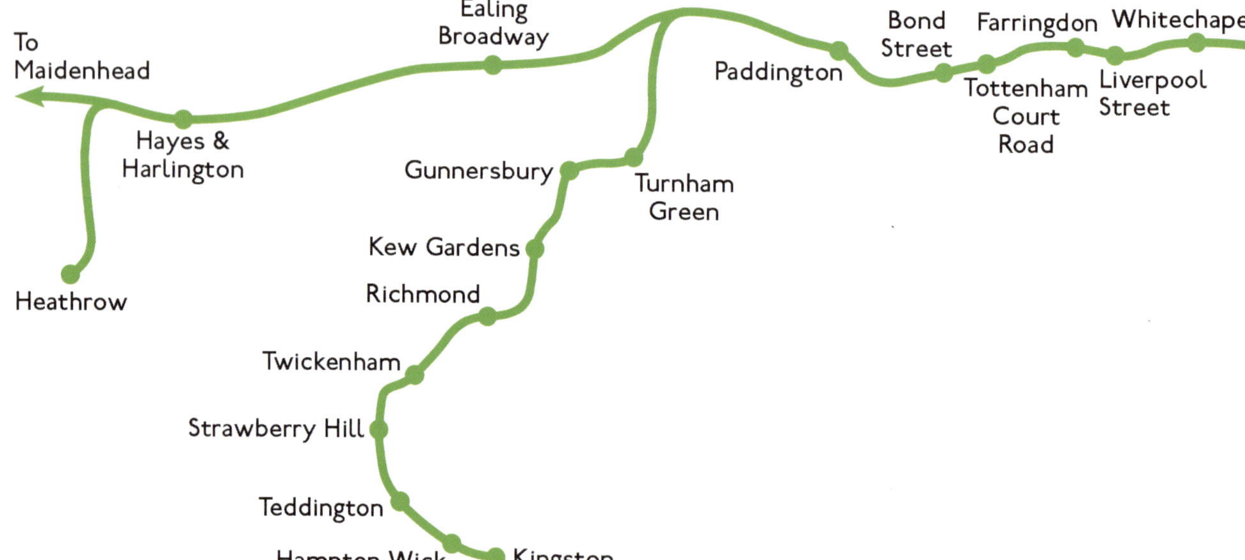

By May 2002, the following options had been discarded by Cross London Rail Links: (a) the route running via High Wycombe; (b) services beyond Reading, or beyond Shenfield, as these were deemed to be too remote for an urban scheme; (c) Ebbsfleet, which was also too far but it remains an aspiration by some; (d) the Metropolitan line to Uxbridge and Watford, which was already heavily used; (e) routes to Grays, which would have substantial freight use and high engineering costs.

The late addition of Richmond/Kingston was also rejected. Under this, from Paddington services would have run at 8 trains per hour via Old Oak Common to the North London Line, Acton Central, Gunnersbury, and Kew Gardens, then by diveunder at Richmond to join the dc lines from Waterloo. They would continue to Twickenham, Strawberry Hill, Teddington, Hampton Wick, Kingston and terminate at Norbiton. Alternatively, District line Richmond service frequencies would be

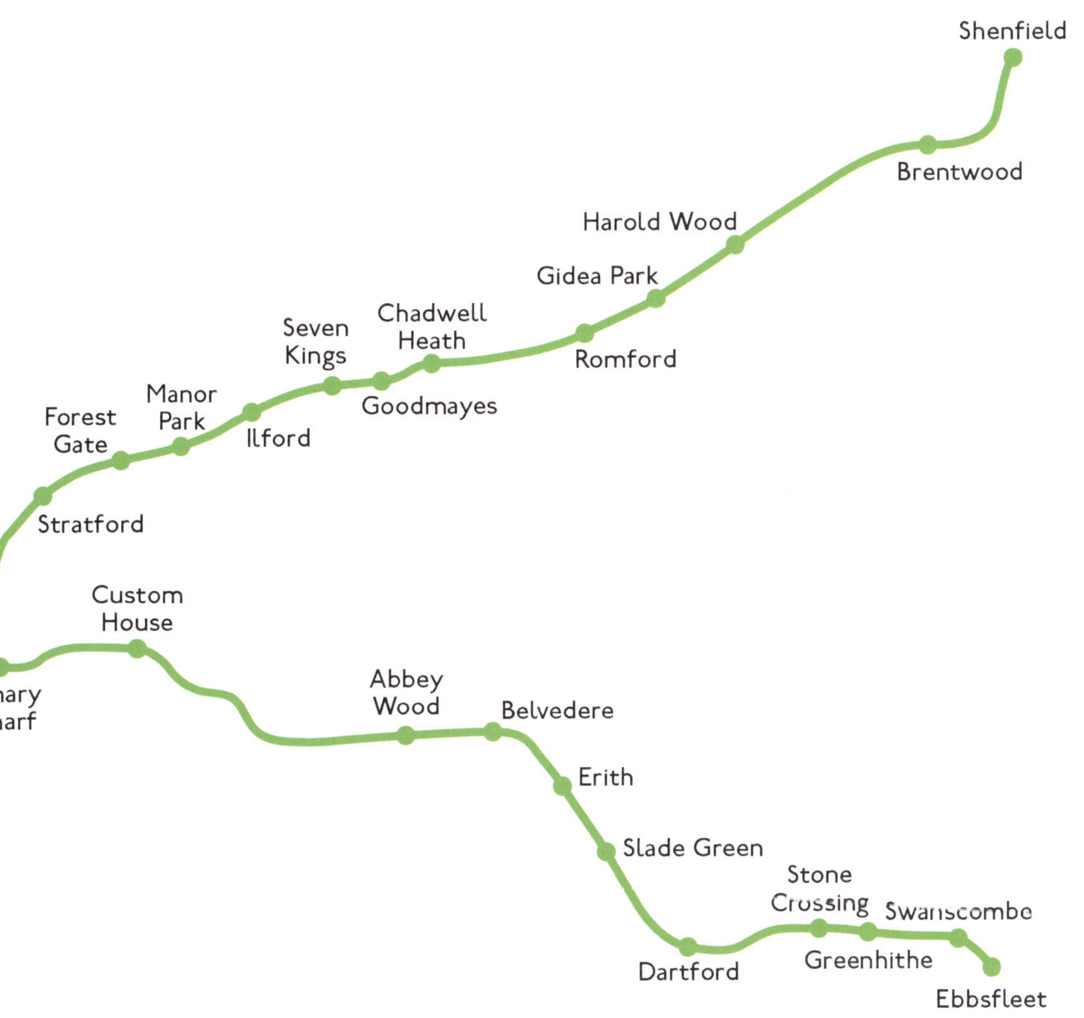

reduced to 6tph. North London Line services would continue as far as South Acton and then be diverted to run via Kew Bridge (additional platforms) and terminate at Hounslow. Other alterations would also be necessary. The people of Richmond had no intention of losing their much appreciated District line and there were concerns about the proposed diveunder for Crossrail tracks at Richmond.

What was then to go forward for further consideration would be:

- Services to Heathrow and Maidenhead and possibly Reading
- Shenfield
- Watford Junction via Willesden Junction
- Amersham/Aylesbury route.

On 11 July 2003, a decade after the rejection of the original Bill, the Cross London Rail Links Business Case was presented to the Secretary of State for Transport, Alastair Darling. He made a statement to the House of Commons on 14 July:

Above Another projected design from the 1990s for an unnamed station.

Opposite The old Metropolitan Line entrance at Liverpool Street was envisaged as being replaced by this new building.

> *'The purpose of Crossrail is to provide a significant increase in the capacity of the present rail networks into and across London to relieve congestion and over-crowding, to cater for the expected substantial growth in demand for travel into and across the capital over the coming decades, and to increase accessibility'.*

In September 2003, Adrian Montague was appointed to examine the various schemes and report on their suitability and cost effectiveness. Meanwhile, business leaders had proposed a business rates supplement to help pay for Crossrail. Broadly speaking, Montague supported the concept of a new link and the work undertaken to date. There was though the polite caveat that the government needed to make up their minds as to what they were trying to achieve, and on which alignments, before firm conclusions could be drawn.

By now, the possible suburban branches from which traffic might originate had multiplied, with six options being shortlisted. They were seen as representing credible alternatives and were:

1 Paddington to Shenfield and Abbey Wood
2 Paddington to Shenfield and Ebbsfleet
3 Heathrow, Maidenhead and Paddington to Shenfield and Ebbsfleet
4 Heathrow, Maidenhead, Kingston and Paddington to Shenfield and Ebbsfleet
5 Heathrow, Maidenhead and Paddington to Shenfield and the Isle of Dogs (variant of Option 4).

Notable was the addition of routes to the Isle of Dogs (Canary Wharf), Abbey Wood or Ebbsfleet and the omission of both the routes going north. A continuing Crossrail route to Ebbsfleet was proposed in 2003/04, but was ruled out on cost grounds before the Hybrid Bill was tabled in 2005. There are a number of track layout constraints in the approaches to and around Dartford. Abbey Wood was confirmed as the terminus, but the route was protected as far as Gravesend.

In 2004 the Government committed itself to introducing legislation to support Crossrail and to work with Transport for London and stakeholders to develop a funding and financing package. A key recommendation by Montague was that Crossrail services would need to be segregated as far as possible from other services on Network Rail. This would enable the hoped-for levels of service robustness and reliability to be achieved.

A Bill was put before Parliament by the Secretary of State on 18 May 2005. 'The route will begin in Maidenhead and Heathrow and travel via Paddington, Liverpool Street, and Stratford to Shenfield, and via Whitechapel to Abbey Wood'. Notably, an additional privately funded station at Woolwich was confirmed in 2011. Reading had also been excluded, but Crossrail's extension there was confirmed on 27 March 2014. Old Oak Common Crossrail station is intended to open when HS2 is ready for fare paying traffic. Preliminary work was started in 2019.

Then there was the little matter of paying for it all. In 2007 the Prime Minister Gordon Brown gave Crossrail the go ahead, with funding confirmed in the comprehensive spending review. The delivery company, Cross London Rail Links, was restructured to become a wholly-owned Transport for London subsidiary.

This time there were no mistakes and the Crossrail Act 2008 was passed, giving Crossrail Ltd the authority to build, operate and maintain the new railway across London.

Construction was estimated to cost £15.9bn, with the Department for Transport responsible for £5.6bn. This would include contributions from the airport operator BAA with £230m, and the Corporation of London with £200m. Transport for London would be responsible for £7.7bn, funded from business rates, contributions from developers along the route and other sources.

The intention was that Transport for London should be responsible for procuring the Crossrail rail services, but that the Department for Transport would be closely involved in detailed service and timetable planning. This was to ensure that the interests of those both inside and outside Greater London were taken into account.

Gordon Brown and London Mayor Boris Johnson launched the start of construction at the foundations of what was to become Canary Wharf Crossrail station on 15 May 2009.

Opposite In planning the subsurface areas of the line, such as this pedestrian subway junction, a number of views were visualised in computer generated images.

Setting the standard

Grimshaw

The Elizabeth line, which in total serves 41 stations running over 60 miles east to west across London through 26 miles of new tunnels, includes 10 new central London stations and the upgrading of 31 existing stations. It is estimated to ultimately carry 200 million passengers per year, increasing the capacity of London's underground railway network by 10%. A line in its own right, not part of London Underground, interchange and alignment with Underground stations in central London was nevertheless a core aim in its planning.

Working closely with client Crossrail and key stakeholders, the project was the result of a hugely successful collaboration between a large team of specialists from a diverse range of complementary disciplines.

Back in 2009, a multi-disciplinary design team – a consortium of Atkins, Grimshaw, GIA Equation and Maynard – developed the line-wide design strategy and for the next ten years they worked in a partnership to integrate the essential components of the line.

Since the line's opening in 2022, the line-wide design in the central stations has become part of a recognisable identity for the whole project, encompassing the platforms, passenger tunnels, escalators and station concourses, and including signage, bespoke furniture, fittings, finishes, and technology creating a 'family of elements'. Three components are particularly distinctive of the Elizabeth line: the tunnel cladding, totems, and platform screens.

Drawing on the expertise of its multi-disciplinary team of architects, engineers and product designers, the Elizabeth line components introduce a consistent look and feel to the central London stations. The design of the range takes into consideration how qualities of light, tactility, sight and sound affect everyone's journey, pairing the impact of passenger experience with practical concerns for optimum performance and maintenance. The application of this 'family of elements' is conceived as two distinct types: the long-life architectural elements, such as the tunnel cladding and flooring, and the shorter life technology elements, such as the totems.

Given the wide range of specially designed products making up the line's identity overall, prototyping and user testing were essential in refining and enhancing the design of the components for manufacturing, installation and future maintenance. Regular material and ergonomic testing was also undertaken.

Standardising certain elements also reduced design and construction costs, allowing more time to be spent refining the concept through mock-ups, prototypes and benchmarks. This brings a sense of craft to important passenger touchpoints like seats and handrails, offering a consistent and quality experience across all stations.

Taking advantage of the sheer scale of the central stations, eastern and western ticket halls of the same station are usually at different locations with their own distinct character. The challenge of integrating the stations into the existing historic fabric of central London also required site-specific architectural responses at street level – a task interpreted by each of the nine architectural practices who were appointed to design the new individual stations.

These contributing factors led to the formation of an identity strategy where line-wide character is strongest in the below ground spaces – where there is the greatest concentration of line-wide components – while the local character increases in the ticket halls and as the passenger reaches street level.

In total, ten components were delivered as part of the line-wide design package: tunnel cladding, platform edge screens, signage and wayfinding, flooring, lighting, seating, poster frames, fire equipment cabinets, handrails and balustrades, and communication equipment.

Below Life-size prototype of one of the corners where the platform and a cross passage meet. It was used to test the cladding installation and access as well as integration of signage and other components.

Opposite The escalator barrel at Bond Street station showing the GFRC cladding following the tunnel shape. The central perforation in each panel is an empty hole, which provides access for a borescope camera to allow tunnel inspections without demounting any panels. These holes can be clearly seen in this photo.

Tunnels and platforms

One of the defining features of the design is the treatment of the passenger tunnels and platforms. At 240m long – almost double the length of London Underground stations – and 75% greater in diameter, these spaces are clad in glass fibre reinforced concrete (GFRC) which 'shrink wraps' the structure, sitting tightly against the sprayed concrete finish of the structural lining. This creates a fluid, vast environment with curved junctions in the passenger tunnels which increases sightlines, enhances the below ground experience and improves passenger flow and safety.

It became clear early in the planning of the project that the long, deep platforms would require two emergency exit routes. This requirement, along with its associated necessary infrastructure, formed the main justification for each of the central London stations to have two full station entrances at either end of the platforms.

This not only gave the opportunity to reduce congestion by spreading passenger distribution along the platforms and within trains, but also provided better station access across central London and informal interchange points with nearby Underground stations.

SEPHORA
EXPRESS ALL OF YOU
SEPHORA
EXPRESS ALL OF YOU

Opposite The standard wall and ceiling cladding is shown at the Dean Street end of Tottenham Court Road station's platform where – uniquely for the tunnelled section of line – the platform is curved. The benches are the standard design for underground Elizabeth line stations; a variation was produced for surface stations.

Cladding and lighting

The Sprayed Concrete Lining (SCL) method used to form the below-ground tunnels at station sites resulted in large-diameter circular tunnels with curved junctions. As the surface of SCL is rough, dusty, uneven and dark, cladding was required to create a safe and pleasant passenger environment – which also offered an opportunity to integrate acoustic treatment and services like lighting and speakers.

The architectural concept for the cladding was to closely follow the tunnel curves to create a sense of spaciousness and smooth circulation. The material lending itself best to this task was moulded concrete, reinforced with glass fibre to allow panels to remain lightweight and thin (between 15-30mm), making it a viable solution for installation and future maintenance.

The panels are perforated with circular holes at higher levels, which allow for a tan-coloured acoustic absorbent material to be mounted behind the panels resulting in very clear sound in the below-ground spaces with minimal echoes. These perforations also house mounting bolts which allow fast and low-effort removal for maintenance.

The cladding system was thoroughly tested through iterative prototyping; this included panel removal, replacement and cleaning trials, borescope inspections, and blast and acoustic tests. Many lessons were learnt through this process which have since informed best practice and applied on other cladding projects globally.

To maximise space in the passenger tunnels, the cladding system provides simple integration of signage and advertising, and supports an indirect lighting strategy by reflecting ambient light across the full tunnel volumes. The strategy defines different environments of the journey: cool lighting characterises the active, passing spaces of the passenger tunnels and a diffused, warmer lighting, integrated into the platform edge screens, creates the calmer dwell spaces of the platforms.

The approach taken in the concourse tunnels consists of indirect uplighting, to create pleasant, uncluttered spaces. An enduring historical precedent for this is found in the London Underground stations designed by Charles Holden in the 1930s, which frequently include escalator uplighters.

← Way out
Tottenham Court Road
Way out →
Dean Street
← Northern line
← Central line
Lift
TOTTENHAM COURT ROAD

Below One of the illuminated advert panels on the platform-edge screens.

Opposite An example of the flowing curves in the subways that assist passenger movement through the station. Great care was taken to design a lighting strategy that could adapt to different areas and emphasise different uses.

Colour palette

A neutral colour palette within the common spaces was selected to complement the lighting and provide a visually quiet backdrop for TfL colour-branding, wayfinding information and advertising. Early in the design the team also incorporated advertising spaces into the tunnel environments that allowed integrated touchpoints of colour.

The shade of purple used for the Elizabeth line was selected by TfL from a very limited range of available and distinctive colours, considering the number used already. It gives an identity that is clearly distinct from the other main network roundels: the red and blue for the Underground, orange for the Overground and turquoise for the DLR. This choice proved even more appropriate when the railway was christened 'the Elizabeth line', owing to the colour's association with royalty.

Despite this, the shade of purple is one of the most difficult colours to reproduce in vitreous enamel – the material most commonly used on TfL signs. After extensive consultations with manufacturers, the team proposed the use of coloured interlayers inside laminated glass panels, as well as the use of screen-printed aluminium.

Architecture and wayfinding

Early in the design process, the line-wide design team worked with the Crossrail tunnel engineering team to reduce the number of different diameters in the station tunnels. This greatly improved the efficiency of the designs and reduced complexity across the programme. Curved junctions were utilised to minimise blind spots and improve passenger flow, and the sweeping curves and flowing grid lines offer intuitive passenger wayfinding and a unique appearance that is rooted in functionality.

The scale of the tunnel environments combined with the long platforms means that passenger wayfinding is critical. Information is 'zoned': onward wayfinding is prioritised on the platforms back wall, opposite the platform screen doors (so to be visible to passengers exiting trains), while digital advertising and train arrival information is integrated adjacent to and above the platform screen doors, visible to passengers facing them waiting to board a train. This decluttered approach gives a relaxing feel to the stations.

While zoning is essential for passenger wayfinding, it also allows for easy maintenance and replacement of technology and architectural systems, ensuring the stations stand the test of time. Technology is zoned into defined elements such as totems, platform edge screens and equipment cabinets to achieve this. Regularly accessed technology elements are also mostly located at a low level, housed in hardwearing, self-finished materials, to provide safe, user-friendly access. Many of these elements are modular and allow a 'plug and play' replacement of equipment as technologies evolve.

Below An early version of a direction sign prototype on one of the totems, before it was announced in 2014 that the line was to extend beyond Maidenhead to Reading.

Opposite top The lower concourse at Tottenham Court Road station showing different types of totem.

Opposite bottom A range of mock-ups and prototypes in a warehouse in Leighton Buzzard, where components were built full-scale, tested and refined during the design.

Totems

A feature that is unique to the Elizabeth line are the multi-functional wayfinding totems found in the lower concourses. These combine lighting with essential wayfinding alongside technology elements such as speakers, CCTV, antennas, power sockets and tape barriers. Indirect uplighting, separate emergency lighting and heat sinks are also included in the design.

The grouping together of technology elements was a core concept in the design of the tunnel environments: their integration within central totems allows wall spaces to remain clutter free and ensures easy access for maintenance in a single location.

The multitude of functions packed in such a tight and deliberately narrow volume to minimise intrusion on passenger space meant that a sophisticated internal design was required. The totems are designed as a slim cabinet with wayfinding arms and lighting on top, with the whole component accessible from the ground and built of modules that can be changed individually. As with the tunnel cladding, the approach was tested first through volumetric mock-ups and later with fully working prototypes.

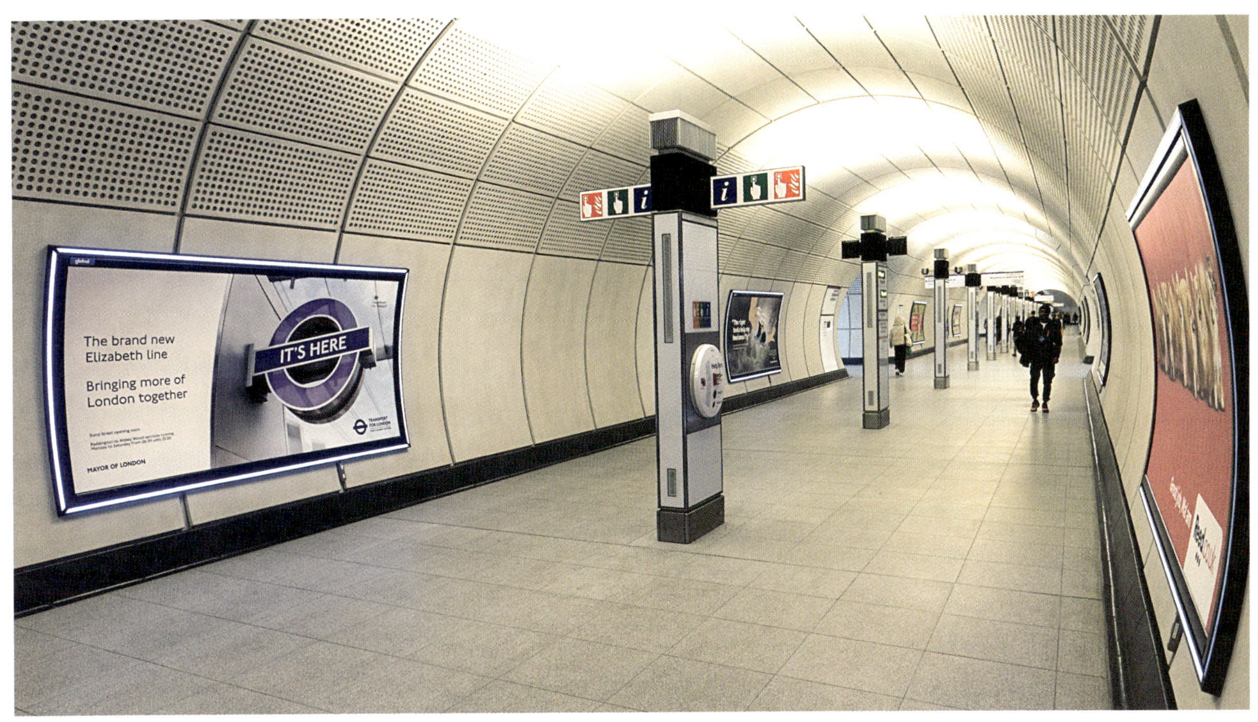

The brand new
Elizabeth line
Bringing more of
London together
IT'S HERE
MAYOR OF LONDON

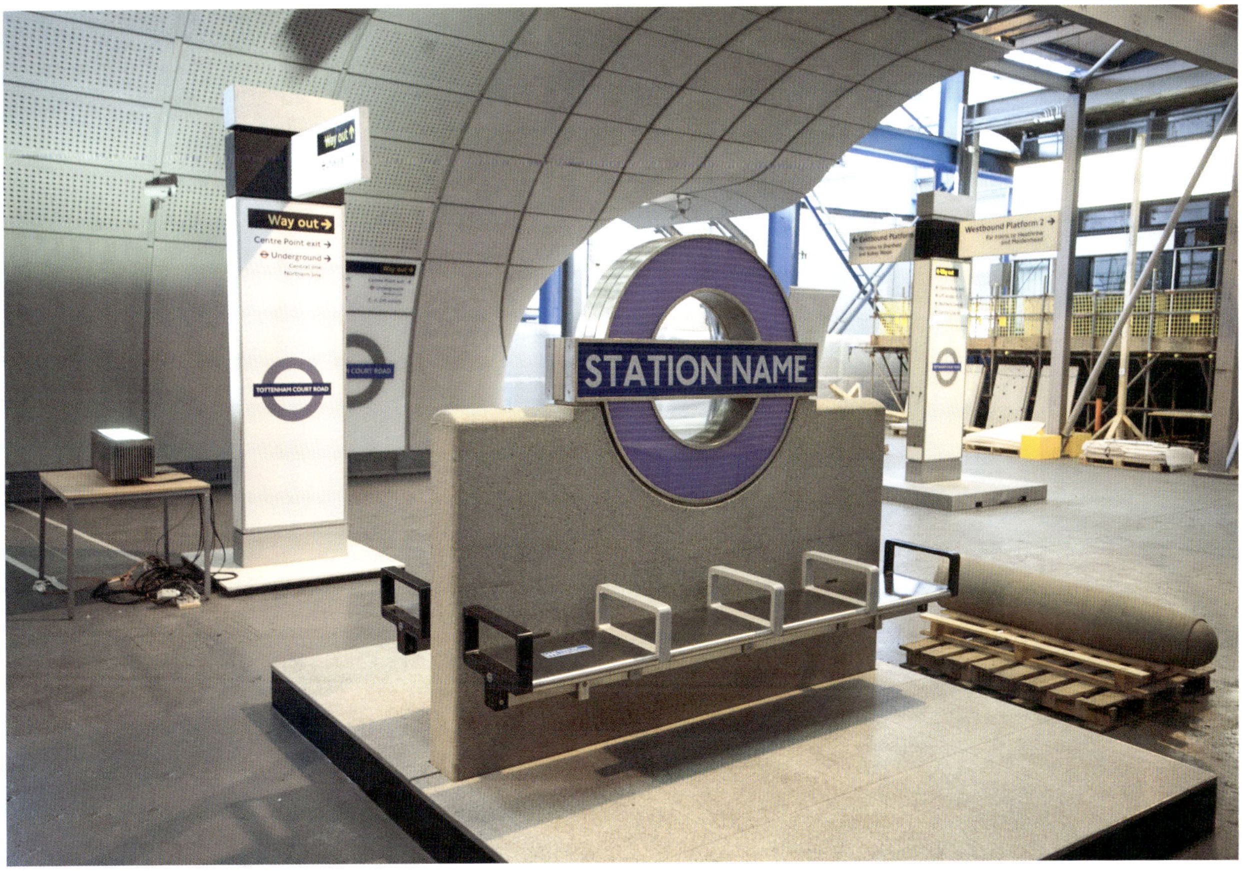
Way out
Way out
Centre Point exit
Underground
TOTTENHAM COURT ROAD
STATION NAME
Westbound Platform 2

Platform edge screens

A significant innovation on the existing London rail platform design is the use of platform edge screens and doors. Although the Jubilee line uses door-height screens, the Elizabeth line is the first use of full-height screens in London. For passengers, the screens are transformative in their elevation of the underground travel experience. They integrate real-time train and travel information through a digital Customer Information System, provide total passenger safety by screening-off tracks and passing trains, and create vastly cleaner and quieter environments, shielding passengers from the piston effect (pressurised tunnel air-flow as trains arrive and depart the station).

As well as providing significant improvements to passenger experience, the screens also provide important practical separation: between platform and tunnel ventilation systems to reduce the number of ventilation shafts required and between the electrical system of 25kV overhead lines and the station electrical circuits.

In terms of coordination, the platform edge doors were the most complex component within the line-wide design strategy.

In-line with the concept of keeping the wall spaces uncluttered, the platform screen houses the main lighting of the platform space, ventilation, screen doors, cameras, speakers and PA systems, and CMS distribution for the station. These components are generally kept black and/or behind grilles, so the overall appearance of the screens is clean and refined.

In the chapters that follow, a member from each architectural practice writes about their company's work on the completely new stations from Paddington to Abbey Wood.

Opposite The 2,300 sq.m glazed roof incorporating Cloud Atlas, a new artwork etched into the canopy by artist Spencer Finch.

Paddington

Weston Williamson + Partners

Paddington is the oldest mainline station on the Elizabeth line, and familiar to millions of people arriving from Heathrow into London or from stations to the west. Designed by Isambard Kingdom Brunel and Digby Wyatt, Paddington is Grade I listed and an icon of Victorian railway engineering – setting the bar high for the design of its new Elizabeth line addition.

The new station at Paddington is the culmination of over ten years' work by Weston Williamson + Partners at the mainline terminus, transforming the passenger experience by radically improving routes to and through the station, and opening up new connections. It occupies the site of the station's former taxi rank, which was a gloomy, fume-filled canyon – difficult to access, and an unattractive and unfriendly start to travellers' journeys in London. In 2012 our company used the future arrival of the Elizabeth line as a catalyst for moving taxis to the north-east side near to a new Underground station entrance, thereby opening up new connections with the revitalised Regent's Canal basin, and improving pedestrian and traffic flow to and through the whole station.

Today, Paddington has a highly visible and navigable main entrance for the first time, with the Elizabeth line entrance extending alongside Eastbourne Terrace beneath a 2,300 sq.m glazed roof incorporating Cloud Atlas – new artwork etched into the canopy by artist Spencer Finch. From a 300 metre long new public plaza, lifts and escalators take passengers onto the Elizabeth line station concourse and platforms below, or into the mainline station through a series of new entrance portals. At street level, a pair of ventilation shaft enclosures, clad with tapering cast stone fins, help to frame the station entrance, and hint at the grandeur beneath.

As one of only two box stations (alongside Weston Williamson + Partners' other Elizabeth line station at Woolwich) the design and delivery of Paddington was a major achievement, requiring extensive deep excavations and complex engineering immediately adjacent to Brunel's historic station in a busy part of central London. The result is as impressive as its construction and, descending to the concourse, the epic scale of the new Elizabeth line station here is revealed.

Buses
Zone I
STOP
1
2

Opposite Departures Road 300m long public plaza, featuring the Elizabeth line station entrance.

Opposite lower 'hit and miss' brick flank wall at concourse level.

The station features a 90-metre clear opening – a unique feature for urban underground station design – harnessing space, scale and light to match the grandeur of Brunel's original station, and creating an uplifting and carefully-detailed space intended to claim its own legacy.

The box station construction brings daylight and natural ventilation deep into the station: uniquely on the Elizabeth line's new central section it is possible to stand on the station platforms and look directly up to street level. Its robust engineering is celebrated – for instance in eight gigantic flared elliptical columns, clad in bronze to head height, which carry the weight of the structure above. There are careful details too – such as the tall hit-and-miss brick flank wall (which also has an acoustic function), the elegant stone paving to the entrance plaza, and beautiful anodised 'lily pad' light fittings set within saucer-like concrete ceiling coffers above the grand ticket hall. The station is constructed on the same rigorous 10-foot imperial grid as Brunel's station, and references to this – for instance in the floor tiling and colonnades – are there to be found. The materials comprising of brick, concrete, stone and bronze are earthy and warm, reflecting the palette of the original station and with a nod to the classic Underground stations by Holden and others. All services are cleverly tucked away out of sight towards the top of the station box, and ample provision has been made for future adaptations.

Unlike other stations along the central section which feature a common design language, at Paddington (and also Woolwich) Weston Williamson + Partners was tasked with all station design from street to platform level. They used their expertise in large scale infrastructure design to create a high quality, calm and legible station, designed to last for generations.

The passenger experience lies at the heart of Weston Williamson + Partners' approach to all design decisions at Paddington. Despite its size the station is nevertheless welcoming and easily navigable – qualities that the practice had applied earlier when addressing the shortcomings of the adjacent mainline station. As a result, Paddington's 19th and 21st century elements are brought seamlessly together for the benefit of station users, and properly establish Paddington as a key gateway to London.

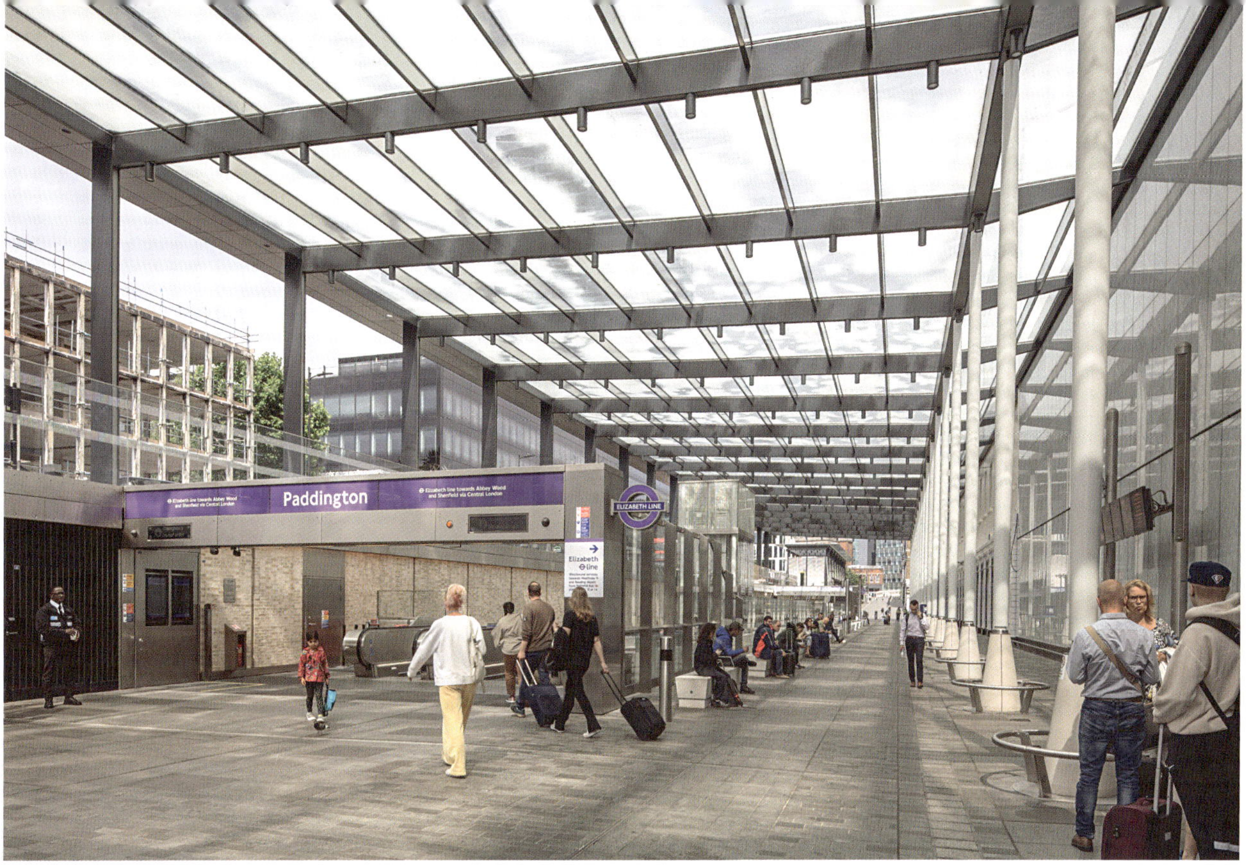
Paddington
ELIZABETH LINE

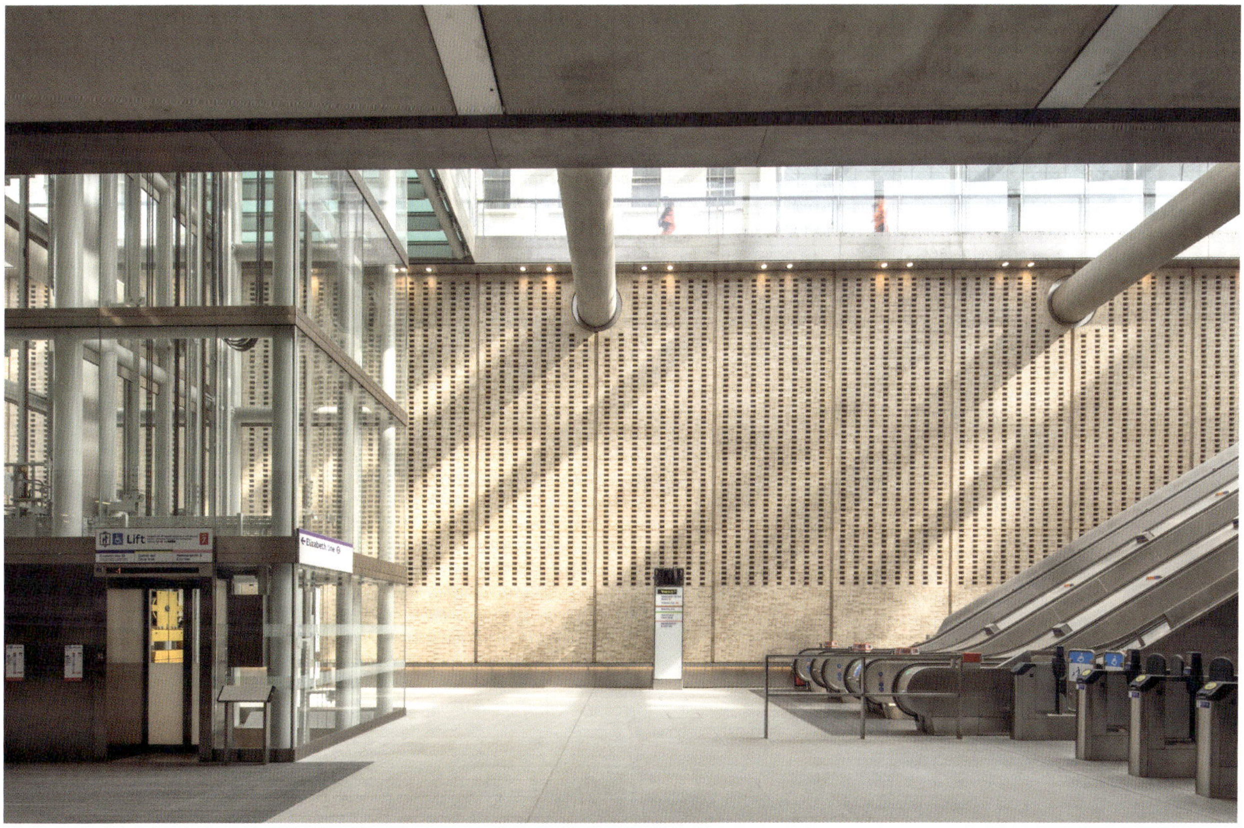
Lift
Elizabeth line

Concourse level showcasing 90m clear opening and central passenger lift.

Opposite top The brightly lit access to the lifts and escalators at main line station level.

Opposite Anodised concrete ceiling coffers at platform level.

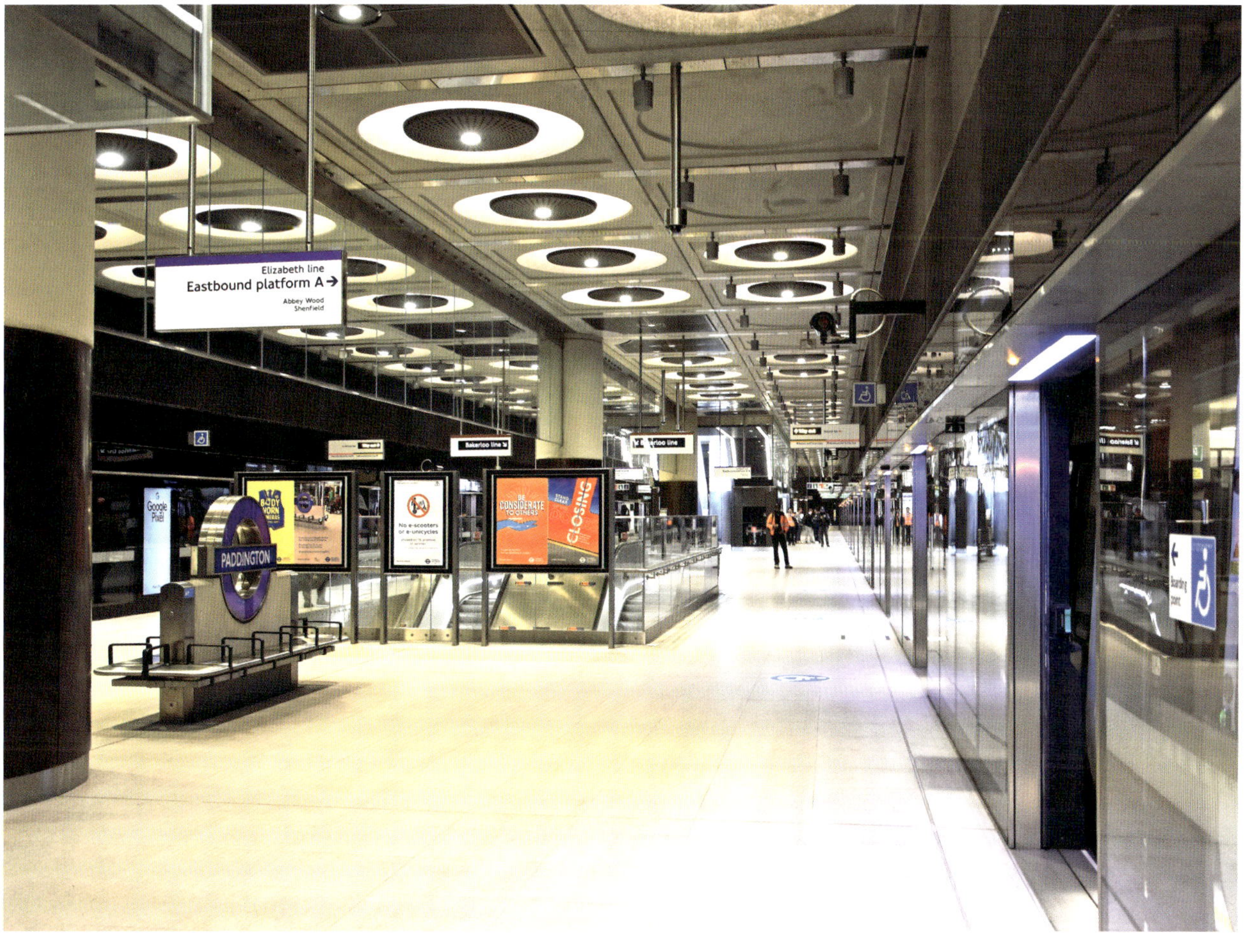

Opposite At platform level all stations on the line share a common look and feel, using components designed by architect Grimshaw and engineer Atkins. In its selection and composition of materials, JMP sought to make a natural segue as you descend into the station between the standard system and the urban context of each ticket hall.

Bond Street

John McAslan + Partners

Bond Street station marks the point where the Elizabeth line arrives in the heart of London's West End. It is the gateway to the prime retail district of London in Oxford Street, Bond Street and Regent Street. A station here first opened in 1900 with the Central London Railway – later renamed the Central Line. The original Bond Street station became a point of interchange in 1979 with the arrival of the Jubilee Line. The station made little impact on the street, despite a modest remodelling by Charles Holden in the 1920s, and is compromised by being located within and under the 1970s West One shopping centre, giving compressed and cluttered spaces unable to grow to cope with the large numbers of travellers created by the arrival of the Elizabeth line, which needed its own station.

Each station on the central section of the Elizabeth line has one or two surface level entrance buildings, each with a distinct identity. At Bond Street, both were designed by John McAslan + Partners. One is on Davies Street, close to Oxford Street, and the other on leafy Hanover Square, a short distance from Regent Street and Bond Street.

The new Elizabeth line station below ground is formed from new twin bore tunnels and platforms – at Bond Street the platforms are, at 255m, the longest on the entire line. Passengers ascend from the platforms through escalator barrels and twin shafts to an interchange level, linking to the original Bond Street station, and thence upward to the two new surface level entrance buildings which are separate from the pre-existing station. The radical reconstruction of Bond Street station below ground, to accommodate the Elizabeth line, generated the two entrance pavilions designed by the McAslan practice. Both locations are within the Mayfair Conservation Area, designated by Westminster City Council. At street level the challenge was to design structures that echoed the established character of the historic area to which they were to make a contemporary contribution, reflecting the dynamic impact of the Elizabeth line on the surrounding quarter of London while also being clearly identifiable as station entrances. Westminster Council, Crossrail and local stakeholders had a vital role in contributing to the evolution of the two projects.

REFLECT FROM YOUR SHADOW
Elizabeth line

The character of the Mayfair Conservation Area remains tangibly that of a Georgian residential quarter, with many surviving – now listed – 18th century houses, converted to commercial use. Later centuries added buildings on a larger scale but the Georgian character of the area, with houses of brick, interspersed with later commercial blocks of Portland stone on a historic street grid, persists. It was a natural point of reference for the exterior of the Hanover Square building, which uses Portland stone externally, bronze fenestration and gates, with internal panellised GRC and framed glass cladding to integrate equipment, including ticket machines and advertising set flush with adjacent cladding.

Together with the developer, Great Portland Estates, architect Lifschutz Davidson Sandilands and Crossrail worked to integrate the station within the setting of a new 325,000 sq ft, nine storey development. This involved combining office, residential and retail space around the station, ventilation and service structures – a vivid example of the regenerative influence of the Elizabeth line.

Assembly of the site by Great Portland Estates began in 2006 and was followed by a programme of compulsory purchase by TfL. A masterplan for the development of the site was agreed in 2010. A number of undistinguished 20th century commercial buildings were subsequently demolished.

Redevelopment provided for the retention of a number of existing façades and the careful restoration, internally and externally, of a Grade II* listed house dating from the 1780s at 20 Hanover Square. A later extension to the house was demolished to create a new public courtyard, the first of its kind in London in two centuries, accessed by an arcade from New Bond Street, at the heart of the development. It exemplifies the degree to which the Elizabeth line has enriched London. The station and associated developments have created new surface level connections and linkages, complementing the Elizabeth line's prime function as a high-frequency hybrid commuter rail and rapid transit system crossing the capital.

Opposite Bond Street station is served by two entrances 300 metres apart. The Eastern Ticket Hall on Hanover Square forms the base of a new office building. The Portland stone-framed entrance reflects the Georgian origins of Hanover Square.

Above The eastern ticket hall at Bond Street has, in common with the western one, a colonnaded entrance leading to the ticket barriers and escalators.The western entrance is built into large office building.

Opposite In the Western Ticket Hall on Davies Street, a high coffered ceiling, daylight from bronze-framed windows and markings in the terrazzo floor all work to aid intuitive passenger orientation.

At Davies Street, with its tight urban context, close to Oxford Street and Grosvenor Square, and set within a new 65,000 sq ft office building designed by PLP Architecture, the station makes use of red sandstone externally, a natural response referencing the predominance of red brick and terracotta in the vicinity. Tall bronze gates and detailing on an appropriate scale give grandeur to the station entrance. Internally, the two new entrances provide a dramatic contrast to the familiar, claustrophobic, cramped ticket halls of the Underground. The emphasis is on intuitive, wayfinding space and ease of movement for users, with clear connections to the surrounding area and within the station itself. In a typical central London station, such as the pre-existing Central and Jubilee Line ticket hall, the traveller is in a confined space, with no views out to the surrounding streets. The transformed Elizabeth line Bond Street, in contrast, provides a radically new experience – both entrance pavilions, open on two side to the street, are elegant and spacious internally. That at Hanover Square features floor to ceiling windows, flooding the interiors with natural light. The internal spaces are lofty, with a generous use of traditional materials – below coffered ceilings, housing lighting and acoustic equipment, fluted bronze-clad columns and terrazzo floors (laid in a staggered bond and featuring a regular band of darker tiles following the structural grid above) subtly recall the Holden stations of the last century and equally celebrate the engineering of the line. There is a clear sense of direction for travellers from street to platform and train, with spaces visually connected as travellers move down onto the platforms, with the deep, tunnelled spaces using the design language common to the central stations on the Elizabeth line.

The Davies Street gateway to the line also includes the sub-surface interchange concourse, providing direct links with both the Central and Jubilee lines. As one descends from the surface level entrance pavilion, the interchange box gradually reveals a richly articulated soffit of bronze acoustic panelling with richly articulated bronze detailing around the openings as well as the integrated art works which serve to lift the experience of the everyday commute. The experience of travel is transformed slowly as the traveller descends the escalator with the play of light in the entrance spaces gradually revealed.

Left Darren Almond's artwork Horizon Line sits situated high above the escalators descending down to the underground from the Western Ticket Hall.

Opposite View of the escalators ascending to Bond Street station's Western Ticket Hall with Time Line artwork by Darren Almond, 2017, commissioned as part of The Crossrail Art Programme. Courtesy of the artist and White Cube.

A key element of the brief was the inclusion of art works, developed at an early stage of the project and considered a vital element in the traveller's experience of the Elizabeth line. Supported by Selfridges, one of the leading retailers in the West End, the City of London Corporation and gallery partner White Cube, artist Darren Almond was commissioned to produce three works for installation in the western ticket hall – 'Horizon Line', 'Shadow Line', and 'Time Line', which collectively form a meditation on the mechanics of time and space. 'Horizon Line' consists of 144 hand-polished tiles set above the entrance to the escalators, at 60m the longest on the Elizabeth line. 'Shadow Line' and 'Time Line' are conceived as a memory of the nameplates once applied to steam locomotives and are set above the escalators, to be read by passengers on their passage through the station. These works are notable for their clear integration into the architecture and physical fabric of the station.

FROM
UNDER
THE
GLACIER
15
16

Tottenham Court Road

Hawkins\Brown

Our involvement with Tottenham Court Road station began in 1992, originally working for Crossrail, leading the design team through planning stages. Then for London Underground to help deliver the Northern line upgrade project, followed by past 10 years bringing it all together with the newly opened Elizabeth line station.

Tottenham Court Road is a fantastic example of collaboration and integration, a station complex straddling two London boroughs – Camden and Westminster – and receiving the blessing of both for a generous new ticket hall, which provides the plinth for a prime residential and commercial development to rise above it.

The choice of materials was key; the Elizabeth line is made to last with minimal maintenance. The civil spaces, tunnels and station boxes are designed with a 120-year lifespan in mind, and each station's internal fabric will still look good into the 2070s and maybe beyond.

The vision for Tottenham Court Road station was to ensure that it functions as one transport interchange, creating seamless connections between Underground lines and the Elizabeth line, with accessibility for all.

Opposite top The Elizabeth line's central London stations are the foundation stones for some of the city's most high-profile real estate. We brought our experience of building both residential and commercial spaces to the development above the new western ticket hall in Dean Street, maximising its design potential and delivering 92 new homes and flagship retail spaces. Overlooking Oxford Street, the first apartment building is a striking six storey Art Deco landmark, inspired by Lutyens' 1938 Pantheon building further along Oxford Street, with a glass and polished black reconstituted stone façade and gold decorative panelling. Inside will be 69 studios, one-, two- and three-bedroom apartments, complete with a flagship 7,989 sq ft Oxford Street retail unit and separate ground floor entrance to the Dean Street ticket hall. On Dean Street, the second five storey apartment building is inspired by the Georgian townhouses of Soho, with a traditional style ground level glazed brick façade, recessed balconies, light textured brickwork and decorative cladding. Most properties will also have a private balcony, a winter garden and/or a terrace.

Opposite bottom Inside the Dean Street ticket hall.

The scale, together with its central London location in the heart of commercial, shopping and theatre districts, meant it had to be designed to accommodate one of the largest capacities of any station on the new line – up to 200,000 per day.

We also had to knit the complex engineering into the city's fabric. Apart from having to negotiate and connect with the Northern line and Central line tunnels, the Elizabeth line tunnels also had to steer clear of the existing services and underground paraphernalia of the inner city, including the foundations of the iconic Centre Point tower.

On top of that, we had the additional challenge of keeping the existing Underground station operational throughout construction. The Underground station upgrade was completed in 2016, including a new eastern ticket hall – six times larger than the original – which has massively improved the comfort of travellers. With it came new entrances to all sides of St Giles Circus, more escalators, and improved passageways and platforms.

We collaborated with world-renowned artist Daniel Buren to create one of the largest permanent art installations found in any transport environment. Buren, known for his Op art style geometric shapes and stripes, worked with us for more than a decade to realize Diamonds and Circles, a permanent in situ artwork brought to life by the movement of people through the station.

As the Elizabeth line platforms run for nearly a quarter of a mile allowing people to move from St Giles Plaza to Covent Garden in the centre of Soho, the design of the new entrances needed to reflect these different areas. To ensure that travellers could intuitively navigate their way through this space, we carefully selected a material palette and use of colour that references the station's locality, adding both visual and cultural markers within the station.

At St Giles, the Underground ticket hall links to the eastern entrance of the Elizabeth line with Daniel Buren's bold shapes reflecting the mid-century aesthetic of Centre Point. More of his black and white artworks act as wayfinding.

The light-fittings at Tottenham Court Road nod to the stage lighting of Soho's many theatres. Designed by Hawkins\Brown they appear to float through the space in both the eastern and western ticket halls. The perforated metal drum fittings acoustically attenuate the space, absorbing background noise which would otherwise make station announcements inaudible (station communications systems are built inside some of them). The lights are placed playfully on the station soffits, mimicking the flow of passengers through the station. The 'wayfinding' black and white graphics by Hawkins\Brown are seen in both photos.

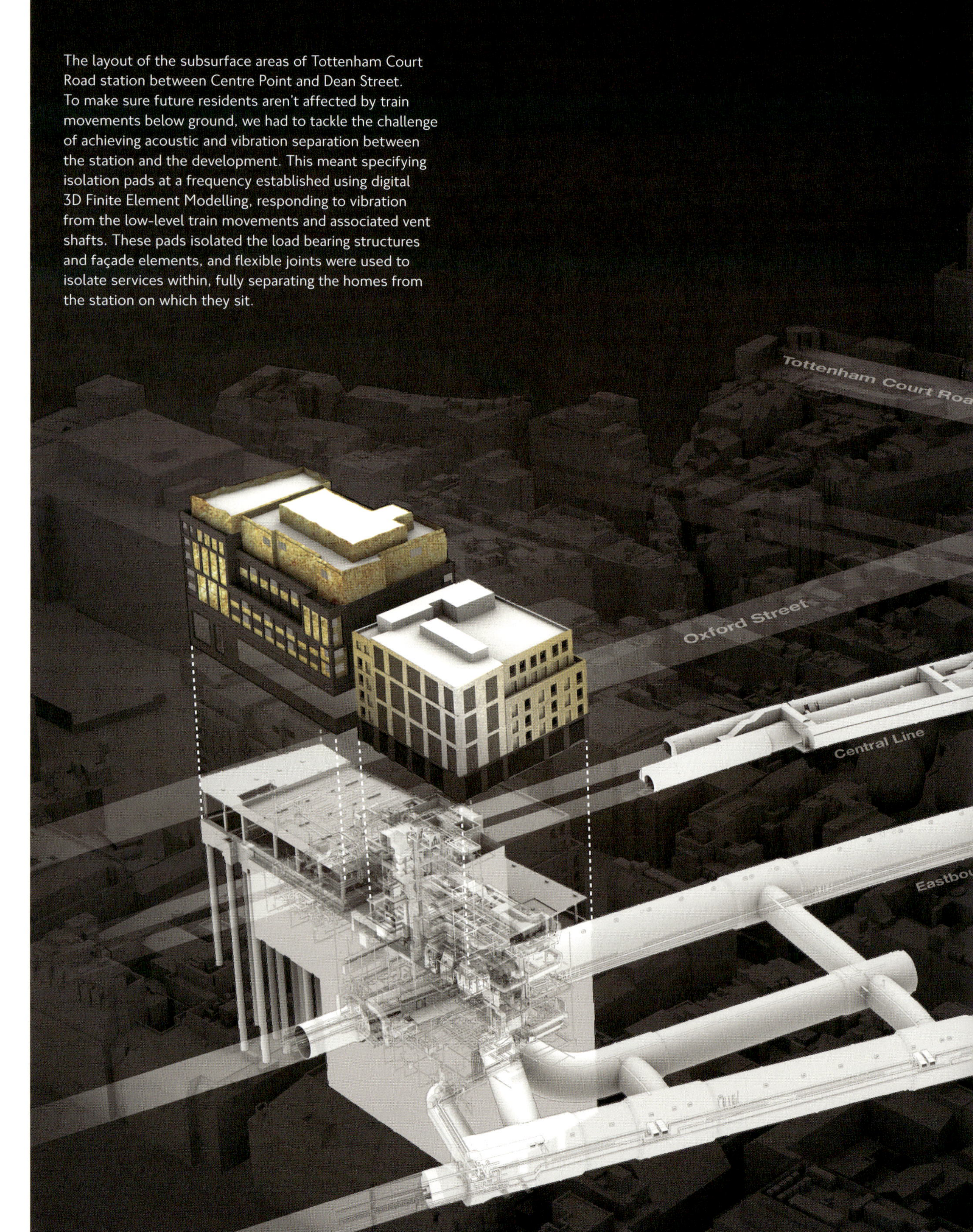

The layout of the subsurface areas of Tottenham Court Road station between Centre Point and Dean Street. To make sure future residents aren't affected by train movements below ground, we had to tackle the challenge of achieving acoustic and vibration separation between the station and the development. This meant specifying isolation pads at a frequency established using digital 3D Finite Element Modelling, responding to vibration from the low-level train movements and associated vent shafts. These pads isolated the load bearing structures and façade elements, and flexible joints were used to isolate services within, fully separating the homes from the station on which they sit.

Charing Cross Road
atform
Northern Line
Westbound platform

Below The gold leaf ceiling artwork by Richard Wright on the escalator shaft at Tottenham Court Road eastern entrance.

Opposite The escalator shaft to the eastern ticket hall.

More art is evident with the Crossrail art programme in the eastern escalator boxes, which have ceilings richly decorated in gold leaf by Turner Prize winner Richard Wright, contrasting with the surrounding austere concrete surfaces.

At the bottom of the escalators, passengers find themselves in a generous space, strongly defined by a diagonal wall faced in rich red glass panels, which guides the flow of people to the Northern line to its left and towards the entrance into the Elizabeth line platforms to the right. The randomised pattern on the red glass, designed by us, is based on the Soho street plan.

The western Dean Street ticket hall uses a darker palette to instil a more cinematic character that reflects Soho's personality. Exquisite Corpse, by another Turner Prize winner Douglas Gordon, is a series of huge screens displaying images that evoke the area's history, culture, and character.

Our architects worked closely with our interior designer team from the outset, not just to please the eye, but to point the way ahead. The use of a varied colour palette inside the station aids wayfinding, helping passengers pass through swiftly.

St Giles and Soho are two of London's most energetic and original neighbourhoods. We really wanted to make visual connections between the Elizabeth line entrances and the station interiors below, and the area's distinctive characteristics up above.

The east entrance in St Giles is white and bright to reflect the 1960s iconography of the landmark Centre Point; the west entrance in Soho is shiny, black, and cinematic, reflecting the abundant nightlife all around. Outside, there are attractive and buzzing new public plazas at the foot of the iconic Centre Point, where people gather, ready for a night out or a shopping spree on Oxford Street, completing the work that Hawkins\Brown originally masterplanned in 1992.

Building beneath a city is expensive. Engaging with the entire construction supply chain is particularly important. Alongside multi-disciplinary engineering teams, we pioneered 3D software that co-ordinated the design process cost effectively. Pushing technology also defined the most efficient construction methodology for structures comprising largely of prefabricated components.

Offsite fabrication of multiple components guaranteed consistent quality of output and ensured that our design aspirations were met, by enabling the design team to flag issues before fabrication and construction on site. This strategy meant 'just-in-time' deliveries, improving the programme and logistics.

Farringdon

BAM Ferrovial Kier

Farringdon provides interchange with both London Underground and National Rail. The passenger entrance from the west is via a ticket hall completed in 2012 for both Thameslink and Crossrail services, though the entrance is branded as a London Underground station. The design of the new station here had to ensure a sequence of spaces providing seamless interchange between the two new systems designed a few years apart.

The 2012 structure, opposite the Metropolitan Railway building dating from 1922, is located in the heart of historic London with a rich and varied history. The site is not within a Conservation Area but is rather surrounded at a distance by three Conservation Areas – Hatton Garden to the west, Charterhouse to the east and Smithfield to the south.

The site of the eastern ticket hall was no less constrained, being bound in a block encompassed by Lindsey Street to the west, Long Lane to the south, Hayne Street to the east and Charterhouse Street to the north. The design of the station's above-ground structures was governed not only by surface level considerations such as the site constraints or Charterhouse Square Conservation Area, but, more significantly, by below-ground constraints, such as the London Underground rail lines and the basement of Smithfield Market, that restrict the area available for structures for passenger circulation and station ventilation.

On the northern portion of the site just south of the London Underground lines is a disused section of tunnel and track leading to Moorgate. This required removal from operational use to facilitate the construction of the eastern ticket hall shaft. When the station box was completed the spur line was reconstructed for use as a rail siding that will be running through the station box.

Given that the western ticket hall has no direct access to daylight, the considered use of artificial lighting is crucial in helping to define the character of the space and complement the timelessness of the station design. A "chiaroscuro" effect (high contrasts of light and dark) is used, as appropriate, to achieve a "museum gallery-like" quality, to emphasise the sense of volume, and reveal and accentuate the form of the architectural elements (such as stairs and escalators) sitting in the space. In the eastern ticket hall maximum use is made of available daylight.

Left The eastern ticket hall adjacent to Smithfield Market and near London Underground's Barbican station is the only one of the two entrances branded as an Elizabeth line station.

Below Inside the eastern ticket hall showing the impressive ceiling and the decorated glazing.

Opposite The public art on the Elizabeth line was third-party funded through the Crossrail Art Foundation and in the case of both *Spectre* and *Avalanche* were supported by Sadie Coles HQ, the gallery representing Simon Periton, with funding provided by Goldman Sachs and the City of London Corporation. These views are of the western entrance to the Elizabeth line.

The design approach for the typical central London station sees the eastern and western ticket halls reflect their, oftentimes different, immediate surroundings. The specific design for these areas of Farringdon station is based on the celebration of fine metal work and industrial heritage of metal crafts that have characterised the areas of Farringdon, Clerkenwell and Smithfield for many centuries. The work of goldsmiths, watchmakers, ironmongers and blacksmiths is celebrated through the station's architecture and engineering.

In the western ticket hall the layout of the interchange concourses was driven by capacity requirements and site constraints, resulting in a couple of interlocking wedge-shaped spaces which the architects developed further into a diagrid theme with its references to diamonds – a nod to the nearby Hatton Garden, London's diamond and jewellery quarter.

A 'pattern' was developed to reflect the emphasis on metal crafts and was utilised in particular in the west ticket hall to give that part of the station a unique and identifiable theme. The Farringdon pattern is based on a polygonal geometry which can be distorted, scaled or overlaid to provide a graphic thread which draws on references to the gemstone/crystal shapes of the main product from Hatton Garden jewellery quarter and the honeycombed walls of the Smithfield Poultry building.

The large public space adjacent to the existing integrated Thameslink ticket hall is known as the 'Apse' because of its large tapering volume, which has been generated to reflect passenger movements from within the space from the ticket hall to the escalators leading to the Elizabeth line platforms. The space breaks down further into a lower apse and an upper apse with a slight offset between them to acknowledge the geological fault and the Old Fleet River below.

The upper apse features a boldly expressed diamond shaped grid pattern in precast concrete with infill panels, also in precast concrete, articulated in a manner reminiscent of cut glass or diamonds. The nodes of the main grid, which feature downlights, are also articulated for construction and engineering reasons.

The diamond pattern is expressed in the lower apse in the form of grooves cuts into the in-situ concrete. The grooves are not simply decorative but provide cable routes for lighting and other services. The nodes are expressed by the presence of down lights.

Elizabeth line 
Way out
Farringdon
National Rail
Underground
Way out
Farringdon

Left View from the 'lower apse' to the portal which forms the threshold to the 'common areas' of the station.

Opposite An inclined lift alongside the escalators at the eastern entrance of Farringdon station. This design of lift is also installed at Liverpool Street. The lift and escalators move at the same speed.

The upper and lower apses are lined with backlit-glazed cassettes that feature artwork titled Avalanche and by British artist Simon Periton. The work, to quote its commemorative plaque, 'is a frieze featuring large diamonds – a giant piece of tracery. The lines and facets of the gemstones complement the geometry of the ticket hall, appearing to tumble down and around the escalators. The artwork has been digitally printed onto the glass panels that line the walls, and was created as a homage to the goldsmiths, jewellers and ironsmiths of nearby Hatton Garden'. Lighting is a key feature of this space with uplighters and downlighters integrated into tops and bottoms of the glazed cassettes.

The geometry of both apses, expressed in the soffits, also has the function of reconciling the almost north-south alignment of the Thameslink services with the east-west Crossrail alignment, and thereby contributing to passengers' experience of wayfinding as being logical and intuitive.

The eastern ticket hall is set out in unison with the building's overall structural plan and in co-ordination with the oversite development. A column-free space, it features an exposed concrete coffered ceiling. The coffers as a whole form a 'T' with the head over the ticket hall and the tail over the escalators and inclined lift. The tops of the coffers over the ticket hall feature acoustic backed, 'champagne' coloured metal panels surrounded by LED lighting fittings whilst those over the escalators are bare, expressing the construction. Though the ticket hall has the smallest footprint on the Crossrail project, it is still an elegant tall, light-filled space. The other walls feature precast concrete and perforated champagne coloured cladding.

The eastern ticket hall was designed to be an extension of the urban realm. Its two external corners are open. This fits in with the detail of Simon Periton's second art piece, Spectre, also a digitally printed on glass. The commemorative plaque for the work which wraps around three sides of the ticket hall reads: 'features an intricate pattern, reflecting the elaborate Victorian metalwork of the historic Smithfield Market directly opposite. Created as a homage to the artisanal and commercial heritage of the area, the transparent artwork allows passengers to see through to the coffered ceilings within, itself an echo of the Brutalist architecture of nearby Barbican'.

The eastern ticket hall features inclined lifts as a means of getting over the local site constraints, in particular, the Moorgate Spur. Another benefit of using inclined lifts is that all passengers – those travelling by escalators and those travelling by lift – start and end in the same locations, so those necessarily using lifts avoid long and sometimes lonely corridors. The brief also included a requirement for step-free access via Farringdon's new eastern entrance to London Underground Barbican station.

Beyond the ticket hall itself, care was taken during the design stage to maximise the active frontages of the building on the site. The ticket hall serves Long Lane to the south, the retail units face the longer Lindsey Street and the station emergency exit is sandwiched between two retail units on the narrow Charterhouse Street frontage.

Farringdon Station lies at the heart of the rail network and has become a major interchange station of national strategic significance. Uniquely, it links the east-west axis of the Elizabeth line with the north-south axis of the enhanced Thameslink line. The station also links directly with London Underground and to four of London's five airports: Heathrow, Luton, London City and Gatwick. The character and overall scale of the ticket halls was developed to convey a sense of spaciousness, openness and comfort: a minimal neutral environment that projects calm and tranquillity.

Opposite Architectural design drawing of the dedicated entrance to Liverpool Street Elizabeth line station next to the large Broadgate development.

Liverpool Street

WilkinsonEyre

The scope of the Elizabeth line station at Liverpool Street as it stands now was developed through the first decade of this century. The vision was very much defined by the significant constraints faced at this point on the line, tighter than those faced by the other stations in the central section. Planning Liverpool Street was one of line's most complex challenges: there is a lot of existing infrastructure below the City of London around here, including Northern and Circle Underground lines, the Post Office railway, culverted rivers, sewers, and pile foundations to buildings. The task of threading new infrastructure through it is akin to advanced surgery. Where possible, the new running tunnels and access points avoid running under existing buildings; the route taken by the line at this point can be traced from Moorfields/ Moor Place, under the landscaped part of Finsbury Circus and down Liverpool Street to interchange with the booking hall of the existing Underground station there.

At Broadgate, we have a ticket hall just beneath street level, and at Moorgate another ticket hall at ground level above the Metropolitan/Circle lines and beneath an over-site development, also designed by WilkinsonEyre. The challenge at both ends was to shape a series of transitional spaces that people want to use, can move through intuitively, feel safe, but also get a sense of visual interest and excitement on the journey down to the platforms.

The sequence of spaces determined by these constraints resulted in quite low, rectilinear ticket halls, moving into the larger volumes of the escalator boxes, followed by the network of tunnels accessing the platforms 30m below ground. Getting daylight into underground stations is always a challenge but it has been achieved here with a glazed canopy over the Broadgate entrance escalator box. Adding value and improving the passenger experience was an important consideration; this includes revising the location and design of the Moorgate-end of the station, which has changed from a stand-alone design to a fully integrated station with an improved interface with the existing LU Moorgate station. This approach made it possible to keep the existing ticket hall operational during construction. The final design has a strong street identity with a blue glazed portal, which is illuminated at night.

The importance of this project meant that we were keen to give both ends of the station, though separated by over 400m, a unified architectural identity, one distinct from other stations on the line. Our solution was to provide a "folded" concrete soffit formed from fine precast concrete elements that span both ticket halls and the upper part of the escalator boxes. These elements have ribbed detail that give an appearance of movement to the ceilings and walls, and create pleasing effects of light and shade, helped by the concrete mix of reconstituted Portland stone with mica to give some sparkle to the appearance. We did a lot of testing with mock ups in different lighting to achieve the desired effect; the outcome is – we hope – a crisp interpretation of the City's historic use of Portland stone to enhance a high-traffic station environment, one that will require a minimum of maintenance over its projected long life. The flooring is a reconstituted stone with a high level of granite in it, known as granazzo, in a shade designed to reflect as much light as possible while remaining a durable and practical solution.

The deep escalator boxes presented our opportunity to be as architecturally expressive as possible. We wanted to evoke the feeling of walking into the nave of a Mediaeval cathedral, with a similar scale and volume, an experience that would be particularly striking when emerging from the tunnels below into this lofty space. We worked hard to avoid having horizontal props across this area, so they could be enjoyed as uninterrupted volumes, with the folded soffit pattern running in from the ticket halls, and a complementary pattern to the wall cladding panels suggestive of geological strata as you descend to the low level platfoms. Throughout there is a strong geometry which adds a richness to the passenger experience.

At platform level, the subsurface Elizabeth line stations share a common language of glass reinforced concrete tunnel lining system designed by Grimshaw. Because this is a very fluid but sturdy material, it has been possible to express the flow and curvature of the access tunnels (adits) and improve passenger flow and visibility round corners.

The arrival of the Elizabeth line has had a ripple effect on the development of the surrounding area. WilkinsonEyre has explored and highlighted the opportunity for commercial development associated

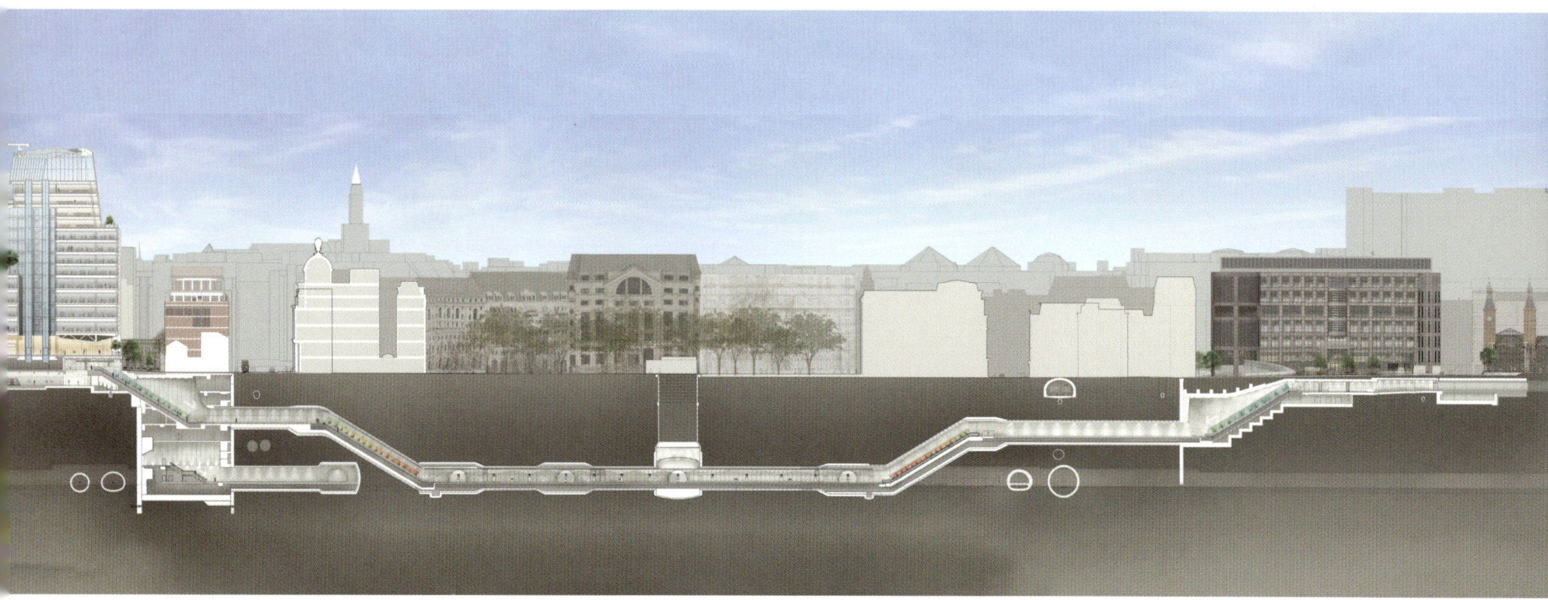

with Liverpool Street Station as part of the early feasibility studies when different sites were explored. In subsequent station design development, safeguarding and spaceproofing for Oversite Development (OSD) interfaces have been included within the station design to protect the commercial value of future OSDs. These interventions include the integration of a "super-column" to found the building above at Moorfields. This forward thinking has resulted in the realisation of a commercial development, also designed by WilkinsonEyre, adopted as the new headquarters of Deutsche Bank and completing by 2023. Our involvement in both these projects means we have coordinated the interfaces between the two designs to maximise the synergy between them to their mutual benefit and enhancement.

21 Moorfields takes the form of a 15-storey bridge, as the floorplate has to be held up by a limited number of piles either side of the running lines (constructed in a complex operation while the station remained fully operational). We took the advantage of being architect for the elements both above and below ground to design and sequence the piling in a way that made delivery possible – the super-pile at the Moorgate station entrance that carries the cantilevered façade of 21 Moorfields went in eight years before the rest of the building to be in-step with Crossrail construction. Other access and ventilation shafts to our station are integrated into the design of new buildings in the area.

The public realm design at both ends has given a much greater priority to pedestrians, and traffic has been excluded from both Liverpool Street and Moorfields around the station entrances. Soft planting and seating were dropped during the design development in anticipation of high passenger flows, but the flexibility exists to accommodate changing urban trends. A public art programme will see two new installations at either entrance – a bronze sculpture by Conrad Shawcross at the western entrance and the first permanent UK installation by Yayoi Kusama in front of the Liverpool Street entrance. The glass entrance on Broadgate glows like a lantern after dark, serving as a wayfinder and landmark for the enormous station beneath.

Opposite The layout of the sub-surface escalator connection between the Elizabeth line at Liverpool Street and Moorgate Underground station.

Left Interior of the main entrance at Liverpool Street, where escalators lead to a dedicated ticket hall.

Below The escalator boxes at each end have impressive walls and ceilings aimed at giving the feel of entering a medieval cathedral.

Opposite Whitechapel was an existing Underground station and remains one, but it needed substantial rebuilding to accommodate the Elizabeth line. Original plans were for the demolition of the original street-facing building and its replacement, but local pressure to retain the 1876 building together with cost considerations led to its being kept. The BDP proposal enabled the retention of the historic station entrance, with initial proposals exploring a new structure alongside the original station (drawings by Robert Keefe).

Whitechapel

BDP and Arcadis

Whitechapel station is one of the most challenging and congested sites within Europe's most complex railway engineering project of recent times. The station, with its heritage protected Victorian façade, serves a diverse local community and sits in a dense urban location alongside a school and The Royal London Hospital. It is an important interchange connecting the District and Hammersmith & City Underground lines with the Overground and the new Elizabeth line.

Following a stringent assessment of people movement and circulation within the station, BDP and Arcadis set out to create a new concourse and its associated links to the Elizabeth line platforms. The station sits within the Whitechapel Market Conservation area, and there was desire and necessity to retain the distinctive and historic buildings constructed more than 100 years ago. A core aspect of the overarching Crossrail design philosophy was the development of a common architectural language for the excavated element of below ground circulation areas and platforms. With these elements providing a consistency across the Elizabeth line from end-to-end, the above ground solutions were tasked with bringing original and culturally-relevant elements to each station.

The final design retains the existing buildings to preserve the heritage and local character whilst delivering a highly sustainable construction solution. The result is the radical reorganisation of this historic site, challenging a previously held assumption that all the circulation to and from the station should be underground.

The early-stage incumbent design for the station, developed by others prior to the involvement of BDP, located a new ticket hall above the Hammersmith & City and District line (HCDL) platforms with access from Whitechapel High St via Fulbourne Street. Escalators and stairs descended from surface level to HCDL platform level and a further set of escalators led to a subterranean interchange passage which in turn led to the escalator shaft leading to the Elizabeth line platforms. The interchange also connected to the London Overground (LO) platforms via a new west stair shaft. The existing entrance from Whitechapel High Street became a secondary entrance/means of escape.

BDP and Arcadis identified an opportunity to relocate the interchange from below ground to above ground, avoiding much of the subterranean infrastructure required in the incumbent design.

WHITECHAPEL STATION
kiosk

WHITECHAPEL STATION
UNDERGROUND
kiosk

Retaining the historic station entrance maintains the fine architectural qualities of the existing streetscape.
Opposite The soaring form of the roof curves up and over the concourse, encouraging and guiding passengers through the levels.

The new concourse, suspended above the London Overground, allows direct connection to the HCDL and LO platforms and to the Elizabeth line escalators. The above ground location and straightforward route enables intuitive wayfinding, reduces walking times and maximises natural ventilation and daylight. The new concourse also creates a free to use pedestrian connection between Whitechapel High Street and Durward Street. The re-use of the existing entrance as the primary station entrance helps anchor the station as a positive step towards reinvigorating Whitechapel High Street.

In addition to these benefits to local residents and passengers, the alternative design by BDP and Arcadis is also more sustainable (with a lower energy demand due to the use of natural light and ventilation), has less impacts on existing structures (fewer demolitions and less excavation) and provided Crossrail with a significant cost saving.

The old ticket hall and station was cramped, narrow and not supportive of accessible access. The new design opens up the space with large staircases and a tall ticket hall with the ingress of natural light allowing passengers to easily navigate their chosen route. A crucial development of the design was the introduction of the curving soffits in the roof, which draw people towards the upper levels as well as giving them something warm, inviting and attractive to look at. This allows intuitive wayfinding, reducing the need for signage and avoiding the resultant impacts of visual clutter. The ethos here was to create something that is in direct contradiction to many of the hard and harsh surfaces common to many station environments.

The materials selected are robust and able to withstand daily passenger use; they are long-lasting, low maintenance and pleasing to the eye. They were chosen to age well in a robust physical environment. The colour palette reflects the local area, using granite and stone for the flooring with concrete cladding, copper coloured soffits and stainless steel.

The entrance to the station through the original refurbished and reinstated 1876 entrance on Whitechapel Road has been retained and the spectacular new walkway alongside the concourse leads to a new pedestrian entrance on Durward Street at the northern end, improving connectivity to the surrounding area. Communities that would otherwise be disconnected because of the presence of the railway cutting through the local area, now have a quick and easy route over the platforms to reach their neighbours, friends and colleagues.

The spacious new ticket office sits on a concourse which has been built on a bridge that feels like it floats above the Underground and Overground tracks that pass through the station. The raised structure perches on steel struts, resting on the brick arches of the Overground cutting. It is set within and celebrates the old Victorian architecture that still exists below ground and the materials work with the old masonry to create areas of special interest. Clear space is visible all around it, creating visual separation between the new and old. This means the design also exploits views between the two levels so that as passengers walk along the concourse they can look down on to the station platforms beneath which are flooded with natural daylight.

In this way, Whitechapel station feels very different to other underground stations and, as with the rest of the Elizabeth line, the character of the station above ground level is based on an understanding of, and response to, the surrounding areas.

Way out
Hammersmith & City
and District lines
Lift
Lift

The impressive scale of the concourse defies the tight constraints of the existing structures around the station.

The daylight, natural ventilation and open environment of the station create a welcome ambience in this congested part of the capital, enabling people to enjoy fresh air and views to the outside environment from the concourse, with enhanced historic features which highlight the unique personality of the local community.

Of course, it was important that the design facilitated the passenger transition between Overground and Underground as seamlessly as possible. The change between the bustling street scenes above ground in central London and the calmer, quieter feel below ground is evident. The links between the different levels are intended to be straightforward for the everyday commuter. To enhance ease of navigation, grand banks of escalators feed directly from the concourse to the platforms, bringing the natural daylight and the passengers with them.

Externally, a new public space to the north has enhanced the character of the local area as well as providing access to the Elizabeth line platforms via three escalators and a lift. A new sedum roof was a great opportunity to incorporate greenery and deliver environmental and aesthetic benefits. It is effectively a traditional roof overlaid with a substrate and planting that will provide different textures and colour throughout the seasons. It works to control water runoff, provide acoustic insulation, reduce the heat island affect, improve air quality and enhance biodiversity as well as enriching views from neighbouring offices, amenities and homes. These measures, combined with rainwater harvesting, solar collectors and an energy-efficient lighting strategy, contributed to a Building Research Establishment environmental study rating of excellent, the only Crossrail station to achieve this.

Another major challenge of inserting an underground railway infrastructure into a city is the need for extensive transfer of air from the tunnels to street level. At Whitechapel, the ventilation shaft on Durward Street is a very large and complicated structure that sits next to residential Victorian buildings and Swanlea School. An early part of the evolution of this shaft was to rearrange it internally so the air movement and the configuration of the louvres directs vented air and associated noise away from the school and surrounding buildings. It is clad in large concrete panels that include a relief design in a series of

Opposite The circulation area to the Overground platforms, and route down to the Elizabeth line is in a structure suspended from the Victorian retaining walls to either side of the existing railway.

Left Another benefit of BDP's 'Station Bridge' concept was creating a straight escalator route from the above ground concourse directly down to the platforms, a dramatic space where the common elements of the Crossrail design philosophy meet the specific character of the unique design for Whitechapel.

dots that form the pattern of a bell peal referencing the Whitechapel Bell Factory, an important part of the area's culture. The tune represented is the 'Whitechapel Road Surprise Major' which was played for the first time, in full, at Christ Church Spitalfields on 24 May 2022 for the launch of the Elizabeth line.

At Cambridge Heath, a similarly large ventilation structure was required right next to the Grade II listed Albion Brewery, which was built in 1808 and has now been converted to residential use. The shaft structure takes architectural cues from the copper vessels that were once used in the brewing process, using strips of the material to create a striking copper façade around the entire building and using glazed tiles in colours such as bottle green, lime and lemon to reference historical drinking establishments.

The entire station redevelopment and the creation of the Elizabeth line offered opportunities which led BDP to propose a 15-year regeneration vision to stimulate economic development and physical growth in the area, one of the most deprived in London.

The Whitechapel Elizabeth line station development has attracted interest from developers and the masterplan provides an overarching framework to piece potential sites together and ensure high-quality placemaking that enhances its character. The policy framework responds positively to the rich architectural heritage, including a wide range of listed buildings and conservation areas, providing design intent for 3,500 new homes, community facilities, seven new public parks and spaces, and a new university and commercial campus which creates around 5,000 jobs. The plan also sets out a more cycle and pedestrian-friendly environment.

The new Whitechapel Elizabeth line station is all about making connections. The design improves and enhances the lives of many thousands of people who use the station each day. It enhances their experience of travel and creates a positive and engaging environment. The design connects communities, connects nature to the cityscape and connects people to their destinations. It is a 21st century station that meets the demands of London's citizens, commuters and tourists. It meets the aspiration of the design concept of BDP and Arcadis to create a sustainable development which optimises opportunities for regeneration and connectivity.

Opposite Built in the waters of Canary Wharf's North Dock, the station sits below the Crossrail Place retail complex.

Canary Wharf

Adamson and Foster + Partners

One of the first Elizabeth line projects to be designed, Canary Wharf Station presented unique architectural challenges. While the construction of most urban transit stations begins with the razing of buildings and the relocation of businesses, this one launched with the removal of a massive volume of water – about 98 million litres of it, enough to fill 40 Olympic-sized swimming pools. It also required the relocation of 572 fish, and one lonely crab.

Over the last few decades Canary Wharf Estate has evolved from a disused industrial port into a thriving business district where thousands of people live, work, and shop. With even more growth on the horizon, the area was in need of better connections to public transportation. As luck would have it, the Estate was perfectly located to join up with the new transit line. But in a zone densely packed with stunning new structures – and with billions invested in new development – finding a spot to tuck in an ample and highly accessible rail station is a challenge. The nine-carriage trains the new line would feature mandated a platform over 240 metres long and the narrow channel of the North Dock offered a perfectly proportioned site.

Not only was the dock ideally sized to accommodate the building, it also provided the opportunity to insert the station with minimised disruption to the many businesses and residences that are located in the bustling area. Feasibility designs got underway in 2005 when Canary Wharf appointed engineering firm Halcrow to explore the station's viability. Adamson Associates (International) Limited was tasked with simultaneously investigating the possibilities for an oversite development and connections to existing infrastructure and gave a unique understanding of the District.

The potential for the development to bring new amenity to Canary Wharf was soon made evident. Foster + Partners was appointed as design architect for the venue now known as Crossrail Place, with Adamson collaborating as Executive Architect on this part of the building. Adamson was also commissioned to design and develop the station, as well as retail space and a promenade level above it, picking up the project from RIBA Stage D after Tony Meadows Associates worked on concept development. Arup was chosen as the engineering firm for the incredibly complex job.

The project came with a number of baseline standards and key criteria; however, the requirement that most impacted the design work was that of the platform length. Crossrail provided the team with additional guidance on its aspirations and envisioned a collection of stations that express a common language, while conveying distinct identities in each location. All ten stations shared a need for cohesive wayfinding, lighting, and advertising space – and it was the intention of the client that each celebrate the engineering form, as well as local context. What better way to achieve this at Canary Wharf than to play up the industrial shipping roots of the area?

Immersed within the dock, the station box reaches 28 metres below ground level, while the oversite development rises five storeys above. The Adamson team likens the 276-metre-long structure to a tall tower, such as the adjacent One Canada Square, laid on its side and dropped gently into the water. While it might serve as a bridge that forges a series of new connections, the building – which houses the station, the retail complex, and a park – is more likely to call to mind a stately cruise liner, floating in the dock and awaiting its passengers.

Opposite Designed by Foster + Partners, the Crossrail Place oversite development boasts a striking bio-dome style roof canopy.

Opposite lower Public space between the station entrance and the promenade is enlivened by landscaping and art installations.

Left A lush garden, designed by landscape architects Gillespies, tops the development.

Below The lively public realm buzzes with activity at all hours of the day.

Crowned in a rooftop garden by landscape architects Gillespies, Crossrail Place boasts a biodome-style canopy roof that combines glulam latticework with translucent ETFE cushions. Designed by Foster + Partners, the roof has become the defining feature of the development and its striking form helps ensure the station is easily discovered. It also adds to the maritime theme – the wood structural system recalls the skeletal ribs of a ship's hull, while the triangular ETFE modules evoke heaving sails.

Curving at the ends to form buttress-like archways, the roof enfolds a pair of restaurants, which are tucked under the east and west wings. Beneath are several levels of retail space, and at the lowest levels, the station, comprising ticket hall and platform levels. The angled ends of the building also artfully accommodate the massive requirements for ventilation of the underground volumes, a collaborative achievement between Adamson, Foster + Partners, and Arup.

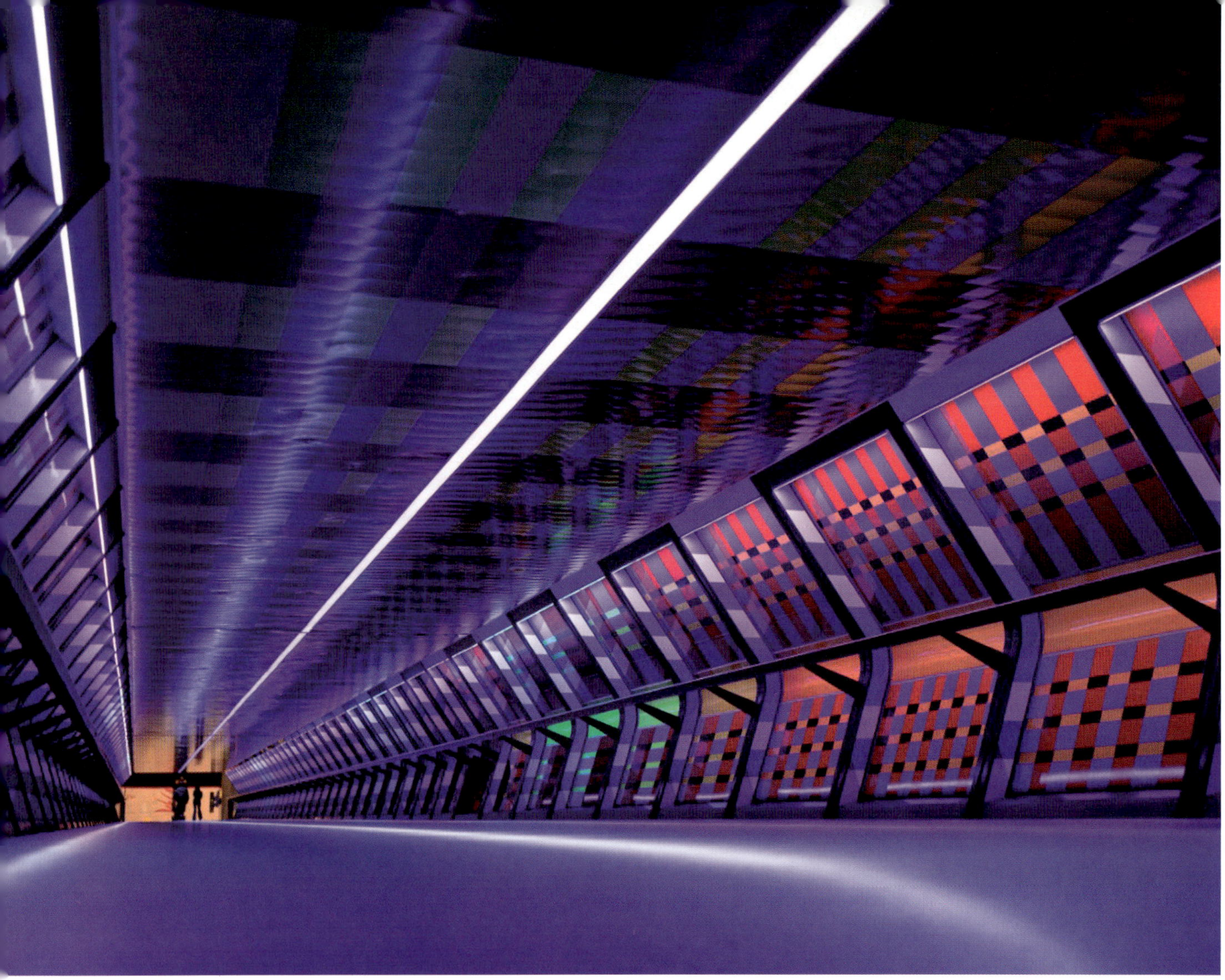

Way out
Underground
DLR
CANARY WHARF
Westbound platform

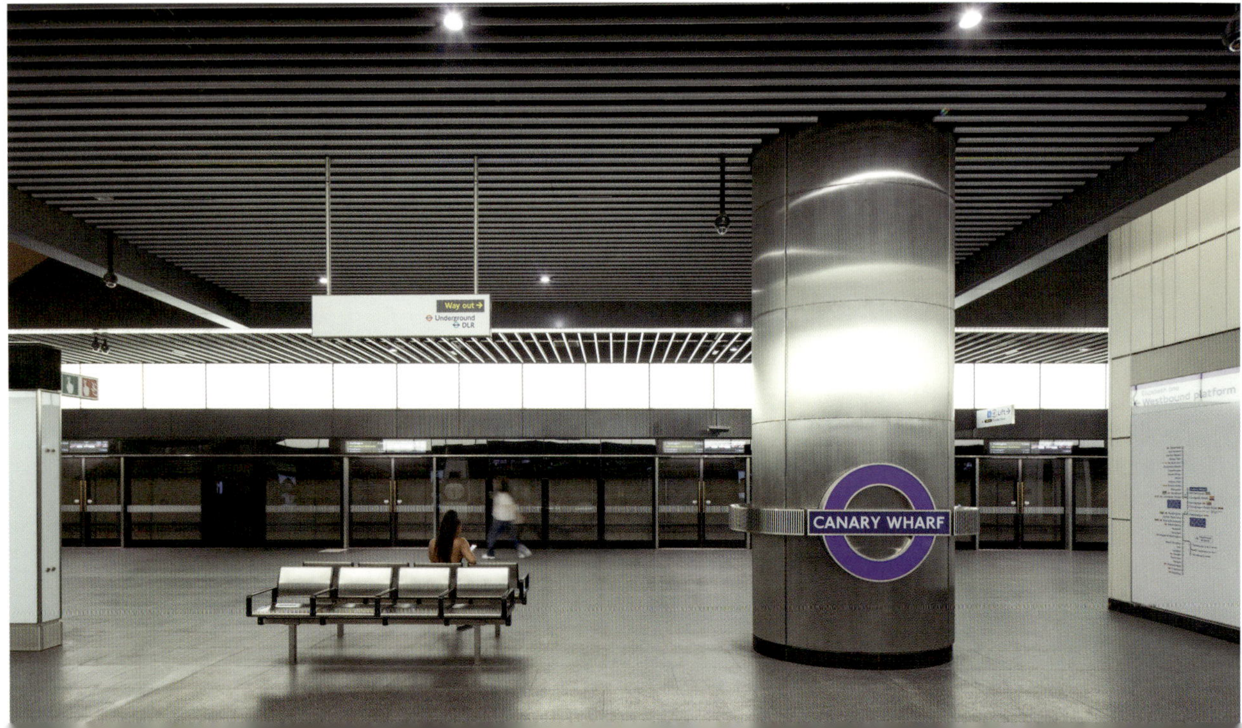

Opposite An elevated walkway links the development to One Canada Square and features a mural by artist Camille Walala.

Opposite lower The wide platform has some similarity to the Jubilee line one on the other side of the shopping development.

Left The gates and escalator, showing the canary yellow branding for the station.

While it may look like a ship, the development truly functions as a bridge. Not only does it provide a fast and efficient new link to the City of London financial district, Heathrow Airport, and more, but it creates a new connection between Canary Wharf Estate and the East End area of Poplar. A key interchange hub for commuters transferring between the new line and the Jubilee line or DLR, the building improves pedestrian and traffic flow to and through the district. Entrances at either end maximise the connections to the existing infrastructure and ensure efficient circulation, promoting a feeling of calm and serenity for up to 68,000 travellers each day.

Surrounded on all four sides by water, the station box was built after the aforementioned 98 million litres of water were removed from the cofferdam, followed by 300,000 tonnes of excavated material. This made way for the installation of nearly 1,000 piles. While many of these were placed in the riverbed using traditional percussive methods, about a third were installed using a nearly silent Japanese piling method. The team worked with foundation structure specialists Giken to install approximately 300 piles using hydraulic pressure, resulting in less disruption for adjacent buildings. Engineers Arup were highly involved in the construction method, which resembled a mining operation.

Though the dock is now used very differently than during its industrial heyday, it is still necessary to maintain an open passage for boat traffic. Each of the bridge connections on the north side are built to lift or move to allow boats to pass the station box. One bridge sits at ground level and links the centre of the building to the main Aspen Way road network to the north. Accessible to large vehicles, it joins to a loading bay that serves all businesses in the complex.

The west entrance opens to both the north and south for easy access to the Poplar DLR station, or the Jubilee line Underground, with a marine deck crossing the water at Adams Place. A pedestrian link crosses over Aspen Way and together this creates an almost circular flow of traffic. A sunken watergarden, viewable from the promenade level, runs the length of the building. The feature adds visual interest and doubles as a flood relief reservoir that makes up for some of the water volume lost with the implementation of the new amenity.

From any approach the development offers visual intrigue, and whether visitors are drawn in from the north or south, east or west, a welcoming entry. Those accessing the station will easily find their way, thanks to the Elizabeth line's distinctive purple signage. This signature colour and Transport for London's iconic roundels guide travellers from the promenade level down to the ticket hall. While the royal shade of purple is the leitmotif for the new line, the design team selected a brilliant canary yellow as the station's hallmark hue, also employed to steer passengers in the right direction. From the promenade, the long-rise escalators are framed in glass balustrades, tinted with this vibrant shade. A noticeable departure from the heavy stainless steel–sided escalators typically found in transit spaces around the globe, the colourful glass nods to the location and brightens the underground interiors.

The escalators ferry travellers down to the ticket hall, a linear volume that runs the full length of the building. Commuters can immediately enter the station or meander through the underground retail facilities, which currently include coffee shops, Marks & Spencer, a cinema, and more. Envisioned as a light, airy, and calm transition space, the concourse level belies its sub-grade location. One of the main design themes of the station is that of a journey between light and dark, and the brightness of the ticket hall creates more intuitive wayfinding.

Many will start this journey outside the station, while others will begin when they disembark the train at its lowest level. The material palette does the heavy lifting on the platform level, with a dark ceiling grid and charcoal grey granite floors – the design team

Opposite The west entrance to the Elizabeth line on Crossrail Place is the one most used, including by passengers interchanging with the Jubilee line. There is no subway connection between the two, though an under-cover change can be made via a subway connection between the Jubilee line station and the shopping centre and then via the first floor walkway between the shops and Crossrail Place.

chose a natural stone because it relates to the materiality of many buildings in the area. Eye-catching colour – the station's signature yellow – wraps both the sides and backs of the escalators, as well as the insides of the lifts, which are housed in columns clad in gleaming white terracotta, a material that ties together the ten new terminals built for the line. These blasts of bright and light colour along an otherwise dark platform clearly signal the way up and out.

Both modes of vertical movement for passengers rise through supersized openings that provide a glimpse of the space above and enhance the sense of connectivity between the platform and ticket hall. As transit riders ascend to the concourse level, the palette lightens, with a pale granite on the floors, more of the terracotta employed on the walls, and a reflective high gloss vitreous enamel used to clad built-in storage.

The platform and ticket levels are uncluttered, with clear sightlines from end to end, helping make the interior a safer, more comfortable and more accessible space that is easily navigated. Simple, clean and elegant, the design also offers flexibility. For instance, the terracotta wall tiles were specified at a size that allows modules to be easily and economically replaced if damaged, or removed to accommodate additional signage or advertising panels with minimal aesthetic disruption. The design team also added vertical strips of stainless steel between the tiles, a visual accent that protects from impacts and breaks the very large and linear space down to a more human scale.

As one of the earliest Elizabeth line projects to get underway – long before the name was even established – much of Canary Wharf station was complete by the time Crossrail Place opened in 2015. Finishing touches were added over the next few years, as the rest of the line came together. By the time train service launched in May 2022, the building was already established as a local landmark which only added to the excitement surrounding the new transport option. Thanks to the popularity of the roof garden, the appeal of the shops and restaurants, and the lively public realm supported by various connections, the building pulses with activity at all hours of the day. Much more than just a station to pass through, the project is a dynamic destination that brings new vibrancy to Canary Wharf.

Opposite The station is principally arranged around two levels. The stairs and escalator drop down from the open concourse to the platforms below. Data comms and electrical cable services are hidden in a spine that runs the entire length of the building above an open ceiling made of circular section metal rods.

Custom House

Allies and Morrison

Our involvement in Crossrail began in the late 1990s when we were involved in the development of one end of the proposed Bond Street station, a new ticket hall located beneath the historic gardens and under 18 and 19 Hanover Square. With this as a form of apprenticeship, we were asked to join a team with Arup and Atkins as their architect to bid for Custom House station in 2012, which was successful. The determination to deliver this project has been there from the beginning and although there has been a fluctuating political climate and commitment it has been driven forward by a dedicated group of professionals to its completion ten years later.

The ambition from the outset was to deliver a world class railway fit for today. The extraordinary part has been the process of delivering it; threading through and underneath a living city with ten new stations and numerous interchanges with existing rapid transport operators. As part of the overall vision there has also been the ambition to generate urban realm improvements. This stimulus that the new stations bring has varied from an over-station development as has been delivered in the centre of the city, to an increase in the land values around the station at the outer reaches of the line east and west of central London, catalysing investment opportunities. Although this is not a new concept, and one that is well illustrated by the regeneration in the 1920s that the London Underground inspired with the growth of suburbia and garden cities, the wider positive impact on the national economy that the Elizabeth line will continue to bring should not be underestimated. From Custom House, high speed access to central London can now be measured in minutes.

However even in this relatively unfettered brownfield environment – utilising redundant track beds in east London – there have been some special challenges that have influenced the concept design for the station. The backdrop is of the enormous ExCel exhibition halls to the south of the station, with a simple industrial and practical architectural aesthetic which makes no contribution to the more contextual sensitivity and scale of the residential neighbourhood immediately to the north. Between the exhibition centre and the Elizabeth line is the Docklands Light Railway Custom House station, and running above this parallel to ExCel, high voltage cables strung between massive pylons.

Opposite View from the end of the eastbound platform looking west. Bespoke glazed cubicles provide shelter with bench seating, good visibility in all directions, and a location for the familiar roundel.

Opposite lower View of the station from Victoria Dock Road. The linear nature of the station and its location above ground gave the opportunity to design an architectural composition comprising a strong base or plinth, a principal elevation using the structure to produce a series of regular bays, and a cornice consisting of the tilted ETFE (fluorine based plastic) roof.

Custom House is a new above ground Elizabeth line station, and as such it does not have to respond to the physical constraints and radial geometries of the central London stations. Whilst it incorporates system equipment and wayfinding signage that is part of the line-wide branding it has other duties particularly in terms of place making. It is also able to manifest a simpler layout compared with the central stations with only a single interchange with the adjacent DLR station connected by bridges from the upper concourse level, and to the existing bus network on the Victoria Dock Road. While the narrowness of the site has resulted in the concourse being located above the track beds, it has given us the opportunity to design a free-standing two-storey building constituting a strong architectural presence in the immediate and more urban context of Newham. Also allowing the overall form of the station to act as an ambassador for the new rail transport system in the Capital, in an area of London that needs some good quality architecture.

Our design vision was to consider the station to be constructed from a kit of parts, each piece beautifully made in a factory and fitted together methodically without too many complicated junctions and components. We considered the illumination of the station an integral part of its character so that within the extensive long perspectives up or down the Victoria Dock Road the station would make its mark both by day and by night. Up lighting the underside of the concourse and edge lighting the canopy above the concourse were both introduced at the very beginning of our concept design work.

The architectural form needed to settle into both its surrounding context but also have enough recognisable architectural presence to register as a building, and of course function as an operational station. To achieve this, we designed a legible structural form using precast columns and beams laid out in regular bays that straddled the eastbound track bed and provided the base for the elevated concourse. In plan this was divided into two unequal proportions. The larger providing a wide, generous, open sided ambulatory to aid observation and passive surveillance, orientation, and route selection for passengers. The smaller, numerous connections via fixed stairs, escalators and a lift to the platforms below.

View of the station from Freemasons Road. Custom House station terminates the vista at the southern end of the road. System wide plant rooms are located behind a series of painted metal panels, and the concourse and station operations rooms above this. A passenger lift set in an illuminated shaft and staircase connects the street to the bridge across the Victoria Dock Road, the concourse station entrance and the Excel exhibition halls beyond.

This asymmetry was further emphasised by providing a large canted translucent ETFE pillow roof over the former, and a solid flat roof and linear spine housing all the cables and operational services kit required for the station over the latter. The natural tapering of the platforms at each end set the limits on the built form possible. To the west this is enclosed to form two-storey ancillary plant spaces and to the east the concourse drops through a double height frame via a wide staircase to meet the platform. Small glazed enclosures provide additional seating and shelters as the platform tapers to the end.

The development of a series of precast concrete components brought benefits to both the design and construction phases of the project. Firstly in the use of repetitious units, manufactured in factory conditions to a high standard, with colour consistency, delivered to site in batches to coincide with the construction programme, and secondly for swift installation using a track mounted A-frame crane to address the oversailing restrictions set by the adjacency of a live railway and overhead power lines. From the outset of our concept design, we established these principles by producing a scale model of a section of the station as a flat packed kit, packaged up like a Hornby train set, which we assembled in our interview for the commission with a commentary to demonstrate this idea. The resultant design has an integrated architectural and structurally engineered consistency; the selection of material and its form produce both an elegant structural solution and an exceptional architectural aesthetic.

The form of the building laid out at the southern end of Freemasons Road produces a tripartite architectural composition. The plinth, or base, consists of a continuous monolithic wall needed for asset and vehicle collision protection. The façade, or middle, has the colonnade, capped by the edge and glass and metal balustrades of the concourse. And the roof, or top, has ETFE pillows supported on slender steel columns. The long façades, both in this vista and as a building elevation that lines the Victoria Dock Road, are intended to produce a classical architectural reference and resonance.

The plan shape of each of the structural columns is a parallelogram rather than orthogonal, with a rotation of 18 degrees. This is derived from the relationship between Freemasons Road and the urban grain of the neighbourhood to the north when it meets the Victoria Dock Road that runs parallel to the railway lines. This rotation is also consistently combed through the floor finishes and steel superstructure supporting the roof. The angle has the effect of altering the perspective slightly so that the calibration of distance and flatness that our brains are used to is pleasantly and subtly disrupted.

The original brief for the operation of the station was that it was 24 hour open access with self-validating of tickets similar to the set up employed by the DLR. Subsequently, revenue protection became a necessity for both systems so a ticket office and gate lines were added to the design, as well as a security gate to close the station at night at the junction with the open access bridge between Victoria Dock and Newham.

Opposite The westbound platform is sheltered by a roof of precast concrete ceiling panels. These are arranged in regular bays set within the structural grid with diagonal, canted coffers that are edge lit to provide reflected light and which give a sense of volume beneath them. From here the escalator links to the upper circulation concourse and entrance.

Opposite lower Sonia Boyce's artwork is integrated into the station's retaining wall and extends along the trackside along the entire length of the Victoria Dock Road between Silvertown and North Woolwich.

In addition to the station accommodation and passenger interfaces, Custom House also contains additional spaces for system-wide electrical and signalling equipment located towards one end of the station at platform level. While these are simple utility rooms we have considered that the enclosures for these functions should contribute to the overall architectural composition, and the cladding thus comprises patterns of plain and perforated metal or colour and white sprayed glass panels, to add interest to the overall piece.

At platform level we have introduced folded planes to the precast concrete soffit panels supporting the concourse. These fold in alternative directions in each bay to provide a simple vaulting pattern that is enhanced and lifted by edge lighting. The materials palette is deliberately simple using the natural finishes to provide a calm context for the wayfinding and overall legibility of the station. The main frame – the columns, beams and floor panels above the rails on the eastbound track – are made from precast self-finished concrete with a high degree of quartz in the finish. The roof to the concourse is made using translucent ETFE pillows that allow daylight to filter through, giving a softer ambient light and are illuminated with edge lighting at night. The floors are finished in granite pavers, laid at the characteristic 18 degree angle.

Between the eastbound track bed and the Victoria Dock Road is a monolithic wall that provides both security and impact resistance between road and rail. In our original concept the wall was battered to produce more of a plinth appearance from which the bays of columns rose, suggesting a temple base. It was to be finished in a graded single colour glazed brick finish. In its final state the overall size and canted nature remains but the finishes have become the canvas for an extraordinary artwork. Here, artist Sonia Boyce has produced her first permanent public art commission in the UK for the Elizabeth line. One of the country's longest artworks, it runs along the trackside wall through Custom House, Silvertown and North Woolwich.
Boyce led community workshops in the three neighbourhoods and collected over 300 stories that highlight individual memories of the people and events that have shaped Newham. Over 170 of these stories are woven into the design of the final piece.

CUSTOM HOUSE
THE PUBS HAVE ALL GONE
If you come out of Custom House DLR station, where the entrance is on the left there used to be The Freemasons pub, to the right on the corner where the hotel is you had The Railway. At the other end of the hotel was The Spanish Steps - you used to see some good fights there on a Saturday night when the drunk sailors were coming out.
You could walk along Freemasons Road and you had The New Gog on the right. Then, you had The Peacock on the left. If you went to the end of Freemasons Road just to your left was The Bulls Head. On Prince Regent Lane, you had the Prince of Wales, The Bancroft Club and The Nottingham Arms.
In Berwick Road, you had 2 social clubs, the Catholic Club for St Anne's and then next to that you had the Custom House Working Men's Club.

Woolwich

Weston Williamson + Partners

Woolwich is unique as the only brand new station site on the Elizabeth line, and as the station with the greatest potential impact on its surroundings and the wider city.

Initial proposals for the Elizabeth line did not include a station at Woolwich, although the alignment passed through the Woolwich Arsenal site as the masterplan was being developed. Work demonstrated how a new station at Woolwich could incorporate the ventilation tower required in this location, while integrating with development and delivering benefits to the local area that enhance the value of the new line.

The completed Woolwich station is a key element in a masterplan for the regeneration of the former Royal Arsenal site, alongside 3,750 new homes and new cultural, heritage, commercial and leisure projects. Its regenerative role means that what takes place above ground is just as important as what happens beneath: the new station with its associated public realm connects it and the area's new community to the wider town centre, and together with a series of Grade I and II listed buildings frames Dial Arch Square – a historic green space that is adjusted to form a gateway to the area.

Thee architectural vision for Woolwich station springs from its unique location within the historic Woolwich Arsenal site and the rich heritage of the former military buildings nearby. The Arsenal had become separated from Woolwich town centre: this building and its improved public realm now reconnects the site to the wider neighbourhood. The Arsenal's military history means it has some very robust and powerful architecture, and Woolwich station responds accordingly.

The new station's single storey entrance building respects the smallest and oldest buildings of the site around Dial Arch Square, and signals the station's role as a major public building. A simple bronze portal with a 27 metre wide clear span provides a monumental entrance that allows this rather quiet building to hold its own against the much larger modern blocks of the masterplan. Beyond the portal is a very calm and simple space, leading people through and down the escalators to the station platforms. Sinuous concrete beams overhead are delicate yet powerful elements and, alongside contrasting perforated steel panels and thin lighting strips, lend visual interest to the space and contribute towards an uplifting passenger experience.

The site supports new over station housing development.

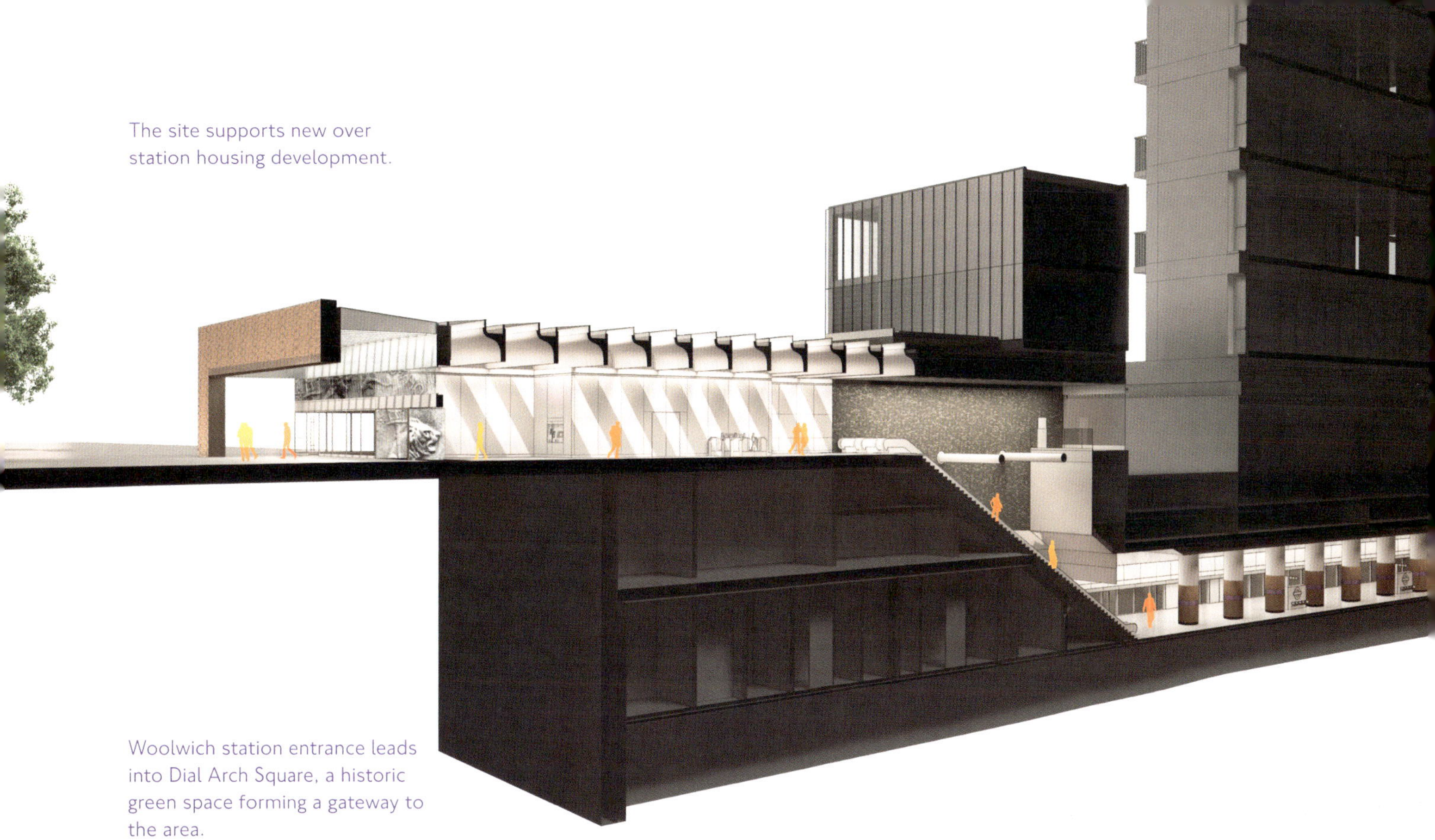

Woolwich station entrance leads into Dial Arch Square, a historic green space forming a gateway to the area.

Concrete beams alongside contrasting perforated steel panels and thin lighting strips in the entrance hall. The detail view shows the integrated lighting.

Opposite top Detailing of the cast bronze panels featuring reference to artillery rifling.

Weston Williamson + Partners sought a robust architecture throughout that could respond to the character of the important former military buildings that define the Royal Arsenal site. This is reflected in the tough yet simple palette of brick, concrete, steel and bronze – while incorporating details that reference the site's rich military history. Perforated external cladding contains images of 'Britannia and the Lion' – familiar from the pre-decimal penny but also used on ceremonial coins struck at Woolwich commemorating the fallen of the Great War. The façade also incorporates over 350 cast bronze panels, each two metres wide and weighing over 80kg, referencing the rifling within the barrel of an artillery piece known as the Woolwich System, developed on the site in the 19th century. Below ground, pillars in the station concourse have a tiled motif in the colours of the Royal Engineers and Royal Artillery – both regiments which were originally based at the Arsenal site.

Woolwich's success is thanks to the early decision to use the line to support the area's ongoing regeneration and to engage with key stakeholders to maximise the use of the site. This came about through successful lobbying by Berkeley Homes, Royal Borough of Greenwich and Nick Raynsford (the area's former MP), and thanks to the foresight and flexible approach of Crossrail.

Opposite External cladding, containing images of Britannia and the Lion.

Opposite lower and below Platform level with bronze clad columns featuring a tiled motif in the colours of the Royal Engineers and Royal Artillery.

Abbey Wood

Fereday Pollard

Below Pre-demolition, the existing station building, the east west rail lines and the vast circuit of connecting ramps had segregated Abbey Wood communities and seen anti-social behaviours set in.

Bottom Early design vision visual showing the reconnection of north and south communities and seamless access from Harrow Manorway flyover, in contrast with the existing station location and ramps in the adjacent image.

Opposite Aerial view of the zinc clad organically shaped roof covering the station.

Abbey Wood, a suburban area on the outskirts of south east London, originally had a Network Rail station building, dating from 1987 and serving the North Kent Line running east west between London and North Kent. The area itself had for some time been in need of regeneration and, combined with local authority aspirations, the visionary Crossrail project was to provide the perfect catalyst for growth and investment and ultimately the revitalisation of Abbey Wood. The new station hub being planned at Abbey Wood would therefore not only become a state of the art multi-modal transport interchange linking rail, bus, car, cycle and pedestrian modes of travel but also be the highly symbolic start of the Crossrail journey from the east.

Sitting on the border between the boroughs of Bexley and Greenwich, the now demolished original station and its immediate surroundings faced a number of challenges which post-war infrastructure modifications had not solved. A good example of this was the location of the existing station and lines which had effectively cut the high street in two and segregated the north side communities and businesses from those in the south side in the process. Without a natural

connection between the two, people had to negotiate a series of long ramps and dark underpasses to access the existing station and to navigate between the north and south sides. With the anti-social behaviours that had subsequently set in, perhaps our biggest challenge was to develop an architectural language for the station and its surrounding urban realm which would sit comfortably within the overarching Crossrail identity whilst creating a sense of place and focus for its local people and reconnecting the fragmented communities.

Numerous other challenges existed of course, not least building a new station complex over a live and operational railway, how a temporary station could be incorporated during the construction process and the numerous level disparities existing in and around the site.

During the early stages of the design process, the local authorities, stakeholders and communities pressed for the importance of a seamless interchange between the station itself and the cars and buses on Harrow Manorway, the vast flyover above the rail lines below. After an extensive optioneering process, the decision was made to set the station immediately above the new Crossrail and existing North Kent Line tracks and therefore at the same level as Harrow Manorway. Connection from the lower levels and ultimately the reconnection of the north and south sides would then be made by flowing and wide external stairs, carefully designed to avoid the cramped and dark corners of the existing station ramps and up to an external concourse to the station building. Accessible lifts would then provide complete access for all persons.

With the design principles now set, the form, mass and operation of the station and its urban surroundings began to take shape. To realise a holistic and integrated piece of transport architecture we involved ourselves in every aspect of the station design including the forensic analysis of passenger modelling. With the new station operating Elizabeth line, Southeastern and Thameslink services, an estimated 20,000 people will be making journeys to and from Abbey Wood at peak times every day by 2026 and half of those passengers are anticipated to use the station as an interchange. The station architecture and surroundings were therefore carefully designed around these passenger movements.

Left With the station sitting over the tracks, an axis is immediately created to welcome and connect the passenger with their journey ahead.

Opposite The flowing external stairs from the upper concourse down to Wilton Road in the south is covered by the overhang of the roof and vertical timber fins guide the eye around the stations curvature. Accessible lifts and retail units are to the right.

Internally, a good example of this is the highly visible curved clear span timber roof over the station building. With the station being elevated on a podium above the tracks, the roof and the internal concourse are highly visible and provide a strong statement of arrival and destination. Once inside, the vaulted roof curvature runs from the entrance to the platform stairways, effectively drawing people from outside the station and guiding them through the building. The larch linings to the ceiling and strategically located uplighting then enhance the station's significance externally whilst creating a warm and welcoming interior.

Formed in individually curved glued laminated timber (abbreviated to Glulam) the technicalities of designing a roof of this complexity raised numerous challenges at both design and construction stages with the technical specification being rigorously investigated. As a structurally engineered wood product formed by layers of dimensional lumber bonded together, durability was vital and moisture-resistant structural adhesives were used. The parts of the roof were then prefabricated using advanced computer controlled machining tools and finished with a surface-applied fire retardant.

The roof's construction – on a compact

Above The covered stairs flow down to the Elizabeth line platforms on the left and the North Kent line platforms on the right. The central curved glazing forms the visual connection with the journey ahead from the inside concourse.

Opposite upper The exterior of the station from the front concourse and the beginning of external stairs down to the high street. The curved internal Glulam roof starts externally and continues inside, guiding the traveller in through the full height glazing.

Opposite lower View of the station, the external stairs and Elizabeth line entrance and accessible lifts at night time from Felixstowe Road in the north. The entire station and public realm was carefully illuminated to act as a beacon of light for the traveller.

site directly over live tracks – was hugely complex. The team worked closely with the manufacturer and contractor to find the optimum module sizes to facilitate installation. Some elements, such as the platform stair roof spans, were prefabricated in larger sections where installation over the railway was required within a single weekend. The project won 'Best Use of Timber' Offsite Timber Construction Awards 2017, and 'Contractor of the Year' Structural Timber Awards in 2018.

Jan Kroes, the project director and lead designer went on to say: "We used Glulam because people can relate to the craftsmanship involved and it works well with the material pallet of concrete, glass, zinc and brick. Furthermore, there was little greenery or trees in the immediate area, so the timber beams bring in a strong natural element to the building".

Once inside the station concourse with the vast umbrella roof above, the passenger will see the ticket windows and machines to the left, retail and toilets to the right, and in front of them a powerful axis of platforms and rail tracks, visible through the large glass windows and immediately connecting them visually with their journey ahead. Ergonomically planned seating arrangements, accessible information screens and wayfinding are intuitively positioned to guide and enhance the journey.

Externally, we wanted the form of the new station building to fit within the surrounding neighbourhood and buildings; the organic shaped roof was therefore purposefully high to create the focus of an internal central

Above The station exterior from the front shows the full illuminated impact of the curved Glulam roof as it creates a perspective towards the platforms and rail line axis.

Left The concourse at night maintains the welcoming feel of the station with the lighting and warmth of the wood ceiling.

concourse whilst sloping down at either end to a more domestic scale. The materials we used are timeless in nature and designed to maintain their quality for generations to come. It was important to create a crafted station, something that was designed for its locality and its community.

Full height and width glazing to the front of the station was designed to create a fully accessible and transparent entrance and to display the curving roof. With the light that streams from the internal concourse through the glazing, night time illumination creates a beacon for the traveller.

Key to the external design of the new station is its integration with an improved, elevated flyover, making it easier for both cyclists and pedestrians to get from one side of the railway to the other. Landscaping around the station includes newly created paved approaches as well as cycle racks, bespoke seating, lighting, wayfinding and newly planted trees.

Unusually in the highly specialised world of transport infrastructure, we maintained our role as station lead architects and designers from concept to completion, a role that saw us work almost constantly on the project for over a decade. We were thereby able to bring the rapport and trust we had developed with the stakeholders into the delivery phase as the design progressed and as new constraints and challenges emerged.

Over the course of our involvement with this exciting project we have seen a lot of change with new businesses, homes and investment in the local area. There is no doubt that the new line and its station have made an important contribution to this and the regeneration of Abbey Wood.

Network Rail stations

David Leboff

Crossrail was perhaps best known as a major tunnelling project. However, 75 per cent of the 100 kilometre route is above ground, and that is where Network Rail came in. Network Rail was responsible for the design, development and delivery of the parts of the route that are on the existing network, running above ground through outer London, Berkshire and Essex; Paddington to Reading and Stratford to Shenfield. The branch to Heathrow runs over Heathrow Express tracks.

From 2014, the stations on the existing surface sections were upgraded ready for the opening of the Elizabeth line. This was an important element for the Crossrail project. Passengers benefit from improved passenger flow and enhanced accessibility with lifts and footbridges that bring step-free access to all platforms serving the Elizabeth line.

The station upgrade work included: new, bright, spacious ticket halls at a number of stations, new lifts and footbridges where required to ensure step-free access at every station, platform modifications and extensions to accommodate the 200 metre long Elizabeth line trains, new signage, help points, customer information screens and CCTV, and new platforms at certain stations.

The reconstruction of surface stations for Crossrail was driven by passenger demand forecast, for the introduction of the Elizabeth line services, and to provide step-free access throughout the stations. The 'Modular Station Concept' was used for six surface station reconstructions on the western section of the extending from west London into Berkshire – at Acton Main Line, Ealing Broadway, West Ealing, Southall, Hayes & Harlington and West Drayton. On the eastern section of the railway extending into Essex, the most significant station rebuilding project took place at Ilford.

The Network Rail Modular Station Concept was an attempt to streamline the upgrading of important elements of the railway. The key principles included the need to respond well to the rich and varied character of a dense urban context, to match the overall Crossrail design quality objectives and a focus on modular components (e.g. ticket offices) rather than bespoke varying buildings.

The principal components were the canopy and the station building, both of which were capable of being extended in modular units to suit the needs of future passenger demand.

Acton Main Line

The new structure built for the Elizabeth line could not be more different from the imposing Victorian brick edifice that served the station until the early 1970s. It provides a modern ticket hall and entrance at street level, designed to reflect the Elizabeth line design identity across the western route. This will ensure that the station is instantly recognisable as part of that network. The new footbridge, stairs and lift shafts ensure that the station is fully accessible.

The design ethos behind the works has sought to provide a station with all the necessary facilities to ensure that the Elizabeth line network can operate safely and efficiently, whilst at the same time making a positive contribution to the local townscape vernacular and reflecting the future aspirations for the area.

Views of main entrance building and booking hall at street level (Horn Lane). The walkway at the rear leads to the footbridge and down to the platforms.

Top Entrance building and extended canopy as seen from The Broadway.
Centre Booking hall and spacious concourse.

Ealing Broadway

The design for the new station set out to provide step-free access from street level to the concourse and down to platform level, improve visibility of the station in an urban setting, give sufficient capacity for passenger growth, and improve the passenger experience and flow-through from street to the platforms.

The station presence has been significantly improved with the development and provision of a strong frontage to the station clearly defining its entrance by use of a new canopy within the townscape. The new façade and canopy design provides significant improvements to wayfinding from the local high street and the adjacent urban realm. This canopy is a continuation of the new roof over the entrance, and together with the glazed entrance doors and walls the station concourse appears to be an extension of the external forecourt space.

The upgraded forecourt area provides good pedestrian interchange and improves the setting of the new entrance into the station.

Entrance building at dusk in a view from Station Road. Structures to the right connect with the new footbridge providing access down to platform level.

Hayes & Harlington

The new station building provides a modern booking hall and entrance at both street levels (Station Road and Station Approach), designed to reflect the Elizabeth line identity across the western route. This ensures that the station is instantly recognisable as part of the network.

The building is constructed on a raised plinth and orientated towards Hayes Town Centre to the north. At the rear of the building there is a short flight of steps and lift shaft providing access up to a new footbridge with lift shafts to give step-free access to all existing platforms. There is a service access from Station Road that visually breaks the massing of the station building up into the concourse and footbridge and ancillary buildings.

The new building is set away from the former station buildings and built to a height of approximately 10m above Station Approach. This helps frame the space and is an appropriate height and scale within the townscape.

Image of reconstructed entrance building on Cranbrook Road used for planning application.

Detail of the reconstructed station building.

Ilford

The previous station building on Cranbrook Road has been completely rebuilt. A refurbished northern entrance onto the existing footbridge has been included along with an enhanced southern entrance, which serves passengers alighting from buses on Ilford Hill. The building comprises a new glass and steel station entrance off the high street including a new booking hall/concourse to increase capacity, with a new ticket office and other passenger facilities. So far it has been the only complete new station building on the Shenfield leg.

Image of entrance building used for planning application.

The completed entrance building as seen from South Road.

Southall

The new building provides a modern ticket hall and entrance, designed to reflect the Elizabeth line design identity along the western section of the route. A step-free walkway, footbridge, stairs and lift shafts ensure that the station is fully accessible to meet the needs of all passengers.

At booking hall level there is access into the building from South Road through to the concourse, with gated staff access around the perimeter of the building to the rear. The canopy covers the forecourt and external access walkways, which provides cover around the station building to the platform walkway at the rear. Internally there are ticketing facilities adjacent to a gateline on the northern side of the concourse, with accessible facilities next to the ticket office. The walkway links to the rear of the station building and leads to the footbridge, which then lands at the eastern ends of the platforms.

An image of the new concourse, footbridge and lifts alongside the original 1884 building.

West Drayton

The station building is locally listed, being a GWR structure dating from 1884, and is characterised by cream brick with red brick banding, has two tall chimneys and a crown of ironwork at the centre of the roof. The southern entrance to the station is accessed from Warwick Road and from a brick-built structure that contains access to the subway.

The new works at the station included modification, refurbishment and extension to the existing station building together with a new footbridge, stairs and lift shafts. The works result in a completely step-free station which reflects the Elizabeth line design identity across the western route.

The new structures are connected to the existing station building by a glazed link set well below the lowest roof height of the existing building. The glazed extension leads to the new footbridge which sits above the railway formation. As a result, the new structures complement the size and scale of the existing station building but remain ancillary to it. They do not 'compete' with the historic structures ensuring the main entrance building remains the focal point of the station approach.

Main entrance building as built as seen from Manor Road.

West Ealing

The new building is located on Manor Road to the west of Ealing Town Centre. The design sets out to positively integrate the station building into its surroundings. The building has a clear family resemblance with those at Acton Main Line, Hayes & Harlington and Southall with well let interiors making use of natural light in daytime. It is constructed with the concourse at street level, with access directly into the concourse from the forecourt. At this level there are staff areas in the northwest corner of the building, with passenger facilities accessed from the concourse. Platform access is located in the south of the building, with stairs up to footbridge level in the southwest of the building and lift access to all platforms in the southeast corner.

Elizabeth line trains

Jon Hunter, Head of Design at TfL

The Elizabeth line should enable 1.5 million more people to reach central London within 45 minutes and increase rail capacity in central London by 10%. The trains are almost 205m long, almost twice the length of those on London Underground, and the platforms allow for even longer trains in the future if required. The 70 nine-car trains each have 454 seats and four dedicated wheelchair spaces, with capacity for 1,500 passengers. We wanted longitudinal seats to help maximise capacity within the trains, but there are also some 2+2 facing seats to give some choice.

Because the train build was such a large contract, it went to international tender. TfL created a reference design to demonstrate its aspirations. We ensured that all design requirements were fully 'baked in' from the very beginning, so bidders had a very clear idea of what we wanted. Once Bombardier was appointed from these bids, another tender was launched to find a design consultant, to advise on the finer aesthetic details. The winner of that tender was Barber Osgerby, a London-based industrial design studio, and the design process began in earnest in 2014.

One of the trains in the large tube tunnelling of the central section, a photograph taken during the period of test running.

The trains are based on Bombardier's Aventra platform but about 95% of the interior was redesigned. The hand of design touched almost everything, from the ceiling ducting for the air conditioning to the colour and grooves on the floor, the castings and the moquette seat covers. We made the windows and doors as large as possible to maximise the feeling of space within the vehicle, ensuring the transverse seats aligned with the windows.

Instead of expensive powder-coated surfaces, there are large expanses of stainless steel, giving a glittering, jewel-like effect, with the line's purple brand colour added to make the train livery distinctive. It was quite a radical departure from TfL's existing rolling stock.

Heating and air-conditioning were supplied by Mitsubishi and based on the Underground's large profile S-stock. A large module in the middle of the roof supplies large ducts and vents down the centre of the ceiling. This system has the benefit of greatly reducing noise and draughts.

Opposite Old Oak Common Depot is home to the Class 345 trains, where all fleet maintenance is done. A second depot at Plumstead houses track maintenance vehicles and machinery.

It was anticipated that the trains would be busy, carrying up to 200 million people each year. To reduce boarding times, each car has three double doors on each side. These are of the space-saving 'plug-type' that clamp inwards to shut and do not rattle.

The train has walk-through carriages to encourage an even flow of passengers and make them feel more secure. Simon Cran, who is head of industrial design and human factors at Alstom (formerly Bombardier Transportation UK), remarked how the gangways per carriage aren't that long and it was quite easy to provide adequate handholds to support people moving through – something the team at Bombradier had already delivered with wide-open gangways on the Class 378 for London Overground and S-stock trains for the Underground.

The trains are designed in line with international standards for people with reduced mobility. Announcements are made visually and audibly. Priority seats are clearly demarcated. There are ten multi-use areas throughout the train, and four wheelchair spaces in the middle car, providing a consistent location for boarding. It also means we have a consistent place to store wheelchair ramps in stations where they are needed, and we can provide information help points, seating for companions and shelters in the same area of the station.

The transverse seats are based on a tried-and-tested product, with modifications to the shape of the back, and the sculpting and density of the foam. The longitudinal seats were custom designed to match the transverse ones. Then there are tip-up seats that are an evolution of those on the Underground's S-Stock. A stepped armrest has been introduced on the longitudinal seats. One customer has the front part, and the one next to them has the one that steps back slightly lower. We've reinvented a design from the tube rolling stock first introduced on the newly opened Victoria line in 1968.

Opposite The full length of the nine car train is shown in this view.

Left The walk-through interiors assist the spreading of load through the trains. Note the strap hangers.

Below One of the pairs of facing seats. Care has been taken to arrange these so that they line up with windows.

We wanted a relaxing and calming interior, not over-bright and sterile, so an early plan to have light-coloured flooring was quite quickly dropped. Dark tones have been used on the floor and sidewalls, with lighter ones on the ceiling to maximise the perception of space. The graphite grey on the floor will actually look good as it gets dirty. This is something we learned from working on the New Bus for London: things have to look very good right to the end of the day. Grab poles are, perhaps unexpectedly, a dark colour. It's really important that the grab poles provide a lot of contrast, but that doesn't mandate a bright colour. We do colour contrast and reflectivity tests, and sometimes even yellow isn't that good, so we use a contrasting colour if the combination isn't right. We thought that a more muted colour could provide a calmer environment, while still providing the contrast needed.

To reduce the number of poles, a new strap hanger has been designed. It provides a degree of lateral support, not tightening as it is pulled. It is hinged so that if a tall customer walks into one, it offers no resistance.

The interior lighting adjusts itself automatically to keep to the right level for the conditions and save energy. LEDs have been used throughout, which should each have a life of at least 10,000 hours. This was the first time that Bombardier had implemented a fully LED system in a British train. LED strips run on either side of the centre ceiling and are supplemented by spotlights the length of each car. The spotlights are integrated in a unit that also contains the speakers.

The trains also have regenerative braking, generating energy as they slow down, giving 30 per cent lower power consumption than conventional trains of the same general design. Care has been taken to keep a consistent theme with the panel shapes and conceal the numerous fixing points where access is required. Fixings are designed to avoid rattles causing noise nuisance in the future. Bodyshells are made from extruded aluminium and have four main sections: roof, floor and two sides. Two double-sided information screens hang from the ceiling in each car, providing real-time information including the time to the next station, connections and any disruptions.

Security measures include CCTV, the challenges being to ensure adequate coverage and evidence-grade quality. Bombardier's team of CCTV engineers were engaged at all stages of the design phase to finesse camera angles and positions. There are no luggage racks or pens for security reasons and to avoid a potential massing of combustible materials. Wi-Fi is installed for passenger use, initially in open-air sections only.

When Bombardier designed the train interior, they looked at its passive crashworthiness, working to minimise potential risks to occupants in normal service and also some other scenarios. Simon Cran explains: "Most of that is to do with with corner radii on fixings and fittings – things you're likely to bump into or bang your head against. We also looked at the availability of handholds, some of which are mandated by standards. For example, these require us to fit grab holds in doorways, as close as possible to door thresholds. We have internal methods to judge if we've provided enough handholds for small users in the right places".

The Class 345 trains are operated on overhead 25kV AC power supply throughout, including in the central area tunnels. Two pantographs are fitted per train. The trains are unique in being equipped to operate on, and automatically switch between, three different signalling systems across the Elizabeth line: (a) conventional train protection and warning systems (AWS/TPWS) on the eastern (Shenfield) and western (Reading) legs of the line; (b) a 'CBTC' signalling and automatic train control system in the new Central section, and (c) the European 'ETCS' signalling system on the route to Heathrow airport.

The Elizabeth line trains are the lightest in their class, at 319 tonnes, despite the high levels of equipment and performance. They are 12 per cent lighter, length for length, than equivalent new generation trains introduced in the recent past on commuter railways. The trains are expected to be in service for as long as 40 years, with a refurbishment after 15-20 years.

Above A train passes through Silvertown on a section of line previously disused and now equipped with 25kV AC overhead power supply.

Seating moquette

Wallace Sewell Studio

The Elizabeth line train seating moquette evolved from the interim Crossrail moquette design which we created for TfL, inspired by riding the route from Liverpool Street to Shenfield, and taking the motif for the grid from a building on Stratford Station. We overlaid this with stripes representing other lines in the TfL network.

We then used the same grid and overlaid stripes for the new design, developing the palette into a range of purple and mauve hues, adding the pinstripe motif to give the sense of speed and fluidity, whilst allowing the integration of lighter tones so that it tonally contrasts with the grab rails.

Taking the grid and underlying composition from the TfL rail design and the royal purple as the starting point for the colour palette, we looked at different options to work these elements together. Purple can be a challenging colour to work with for some designers, but we like to think that we can design with any colour and make it work.

For this design, we added greyer mauves and warm stone shades to the palette to ground the royal purple, plus tarmac grey to broaden the tonal range and then worked in as much white as we could to the design, to create the overall contrast with the grab rails. The white was broken up by the pinstripe motifs, a nod to the pinstripe suits of the City of London, and the contrasting accents of the overlaid stripes to disguise the inevitable wear and tear of daily use.

Once the design was signed off, we adjusted it to fit the parameters of the looms at the manufacturers (Camira) and selected the yarn colours for the moquette to be woven in.

The Elizabeth line design moves beyond the familiar simple abstract styles of many other moquettes, through the complexity of the patterning and the richness of the colouring. The variety of tone and hue is made through the blending the five background shades in the fine pinstripes, allowing simultaneous contrast to give the perception of extra colours, whilst the warm stone shade adds an underlying subtle richness to the cloth.

Alongside this, the intricate pattern, composed of duplicated elements that camouflage the design's repeat, creates a visual richness, which combined with the royal purple suggests a regal heritage. Yet the overall impression of the design is modern, through the use of the grid and pattern system, reflecting the dynamic sense of flow in the city.

Wallace Sewell has designed a number of seating moquettes for TfL, including some for London Underground trains, the London Overground and Tramlink. Below are the sketches for TfL Rail (the interim operator of the stopping service between Shenfield and Liverpool Street prior to opening of the Elizabeth line) and, on the right, the final TfL Rail design – used on second hand rolling stock taken over from Greater Anglia. The two Elizabeth line moquettes (there is a minor design variation for use on priority seating) make greater use of the line's brand colour.

Opposite The moquette in use. The colour palette started with the specific shade of purple that is the line colour, to which we added other tones of purple, mixed with warmer and lighter shades to keep the fabric bright in overall effect, complementing the interior colour scheme. The palette also incorporates flashes of other line colours that the route interacts with as accents. The eye is drawn along the carriage by the design whilst maintaining a vertical framework.

This page A range of items using Elizabeth line moquette has been produced for sale by the London Transport Museum.

Acknowledgements

The invaluable assistance of David Leboff and Transport for London in the preparation of this book is gratefully acknowledged. Many others assisted at one stage or more including Julian Robinson, Neill McClements, Julian Maynard, Jon Hunter, Andy Barr, Chris Pollard, Soji Abass, Russell Eggar, Hanna Selby, Erin Donnelly, Emily Ramsay and Christina Morris. The Liverpool Street text was written by Oliver Tyler, the Whitechapel text was written by Peter Jenkins and the Custom House text was written by Robert Maxwell. All the architectural and design companies were very helpful in the supply of text and illustrations.

For the underground station areas of the line, Atkins was the package lead, with a project management and client advisory role in addition to providing full engineering services with architectural and expert technical advice. Grimshaw led the overall line-wide design concept, galvanising input from the different specialists within the team to produce coherent architectural and industrial design solutions. Maynard led the signage, wayfinding and graphic information design. Equation provided specialist technical and design guidance on the lighting.

ILLUSTRATION CREDITS

Front cover Morley von Sternberg for Weston Williamson + Partners
Page 1 Transport for London
Page 2 Steven Chilcott
Pages 6-7 Crossrail Ltd
Pages 8-9 Mike Harris
Pages 10-11 Crossrail Ltd
Page 13 Grimshaw
Pages 25-29 top Morley von Sternberg for Weston Williamson + Partners
Page 29 bottom Colin Stannard
Page 31 G G Archard for John McAslan + Partners
Pages 32-34 and 35 top John McAslan + Partners
Page 35 bottom Transport for London
Page 36 top John McAslan + Partners
Page 36 bottom and 37 G G Archard for John McAslan + Partners
Page 39 top Hawkins\Brown
Page 39 bottom Morley von Sternberg for Hawkins\Brown
Pages 40-41 Jack Hobhouse
Pages 42-43 Hawkins\Brown
Pages 44-45 Jack Hobhouse
Page 47 top Crossrail Ltd
Page 47 bottom Morley von Sternberg for BAM Ferrovial Kier
Pages 49-51 Morley von Sternberg for BAM Ferrovial Kier
Pages 53-54 WilkinsonEyre
Page 55 top Ben Bisek for WilkinsonEyre
Page 55 bottom Will Collin
Pages 57-63 BDP and Arcadis
Page 65 Foster + Partners
Page 66 Peter Matthews, courtesy of Adamson
Page 67 top Nunzio Prenna, courtesy of Canary Wharf Group
Page 67 bottom Sean Pollock, courtesy of Canary Wharf Group
Pages 68 -71 Peter Matthews, courtesy of Adamson
Pages 73-79 Morley von Sternberg for Allies and Morrison
Page 81 top Weston Williamson + Partners
Page 81 bottom Morley von Sternberg for Weston Williamson + Partners
Pages 82-85 Morley von Sternberg for Weston Williamson + Partners
Page 86 Fereday Pollard
Page 87 Crossrail Ltd
Page 88 Fereday Pollard
Page 89 Crossrail Ltd
Pages 90-93 Fereday Pollard
Page 95 The Graham Group
Page 96 top David Leboff
Page 96 bottom Network Rail
Page 97 Alamy
Page 98 top Atkins
Page 98 centre Network Rail
Page 99 top Bennetts Associates
Page 99 centre Network Rail
Page 100 Bennetts Associates
Page 101 top Bennetts Associates
Page 101 centre Network Rail
Pages 102-103 Transport for London
Page 104 Justin Bailey
Page 105 top Justin Bailey
Page 105 bottom Capital Transport
Page 106 Kim Rennie
Page 107 Justin Bailey
Page 109 Wallace Sewell
Page 110 Transport for London
Page 111 London Transport Museum
Back cover Ticket wallets © TfL